ALIVE IN THE KILLING FIELDS

ALIVE
IN THE
KILLING FIELDS

SURVIVING THE KHMER ROUGE GENOCIDE

by Nawuth Keat with Martha E. Kendall

NATIONAL GEOGRAPHIC
WASHINGTON, D.C.

Published by the National Geographic Society.

The publisher would like to thank Kim DePaul, Executive Director of the Dith Pran Holocaust Awareness Project for her generous assistance and thoughtful review of this book.

For information about special discounts for bulk purchases, please contact National Geographic Books Special Sales: ngspecsales@ngs.org.

For rights or permissions inquires, please contact National Geographic Books Subsidiary Rights: ngbookrights@ngs.org.

Cover design by Jonathan Halling. Interior design by Sandi Owatverot.
The body text of the book is set in Hoefler Text.
The display text is set in Bourgeois.

Library of Congress Cataloging-in-Publication Data
Keat, Nawuth, 1964-
  Alive in the killing fields : surviving the Khmer Rouge genocide
/by Nawuth Keat and Martha E. Kendall.—1st ed.
    p. cm.
  Includes bibliographical references and index.
  ISBN 978-1-4263-0515-3 (hardcover : alk. paper)—ISBN 978-1-4263-0516-0 (library binding : alk. paper)
  1. Keat, Nawuth, 1964—Juvenile literature. 2. Political refugees—Cambodia—Biography. 3. Political refugees—United States—Biography. I. Kendall, Martha. II. Title.
  DS554.83.K43A3 2009
  959.604'2—dc22
  [B]
                        2008039805
Printed in the United States of America

09/WOR/1

This book is dedicated to the men, women, and children who lost their lives under the Khmer Rouge.
–N.K. and M.E.K.

I want to thank my teacher and friend, Martha Kendall, for offering to write my story down.
—*Nawuth Keat*

I would like to acknowledge the loving support of my family, the fine work of National Geographic editor Priyanka Lamichhane, and especially the courage of Nawuth Keat who re-lived the tragedies recounted in this book as he told them to me.
—*Martha E. Kendall*

Table of Contents

PREFACE

Nawuth (NAH-wooth) Keat was a student in my World Literature course at San Jose City College. He seldom spoke in class. So I was surprised on the last day when he said, "I'd like to share my story with you."

Nawuth described his childhood in war-torn Cambodia, his family's tragedies, the constant hunger, and his dangerous escape. I looked around the classroom and saw that I was not the only listener who had been moved to tears.

"Nawuth, would you like me to write your story down for you?" I asked.

"Yes," he answered simply.

Since then Nawuth and I have spent many hours working together. His English is rough. My role is to gather his memories and write them down clearly in English. The words are mine, but the story is his.

Sometimes the going got tough. As Nawuth reviewed the manuscript, he was taken back to his painful past.

I asked, "Are you sure you want to continue with this project?"

"I want people to know the truth about what happened," he said.

Here is Nawuth's truth.

MARTHA E. KENDALL

Chapter One

"YOU'RE LUCKY"

Gunshots!

I bolted awake. My parents yelled, and we all jumped from our beds. The dogs barked.

"We have to get out of here!" my parents said.

Still in our pajamas, we darted outside.

"Run to my mother's," my father said. She lived next door, and we hurried to her house. We heard gunfire close by, right in the neighborhood.

We got our grandmother, and together all ran toward an old rice barn across the street. But the gunshots came so close to us that we couldn't make it to the barn. Instead, we dove into a ditch—my mother, the baby, my grandmother, my younger brothers, my aunt and uncle, our babysitter, and me. I was nine years old.

The ditch was too shallow to hide us, but in the darkness, I hoped we'd be overlooked. My father ducked behind some bamboo about a hundred feet away.

My heart pounded. I heard screams, explosions, howling animals, and the fiery roar of grass-roofed houses burning.

My mother had always told us, "The Khmer Rouge (Kuh-mair Roozh) might come at any time to raid our village. Their leader, a man named Pol Pot, says he and the Communists want to make everyone in Cambodia equal, but that's just talk. It is an excuse they use to help them gain power. Banding together in big gangs, they kill people and steal money, gold jewelry, and guns."

Now they had come: the Khmer Rouge, the Red People. They were mostly poor and uneducated peasants, thieves, drunks, and fugitives.

My mother was so afraid of them; she rarely let us sleep at home. Most nights my father took us to the home of my mother's parents, about five miles away. To get there, they drove motorcycles, pulling us kids in trailers behind them. My mother said, "It's safer there, because it's a larger town." But on this night we had stayed home to prepare food for the next day's holiday feast, the Cambodian Thanksgiving.

Our town had no electricity, so the Khmer Rouge tried to light up the street by starting fires anywhere they could. They threw burning matches into our house, but it did not ignite. Then they used a trick to fool anyone who was hiding in the shadows. They yelled in no particular direction, "Hey, you, stand still! If you move, we'll shoot!"

My grandmother fell for it. Terrified, afraid the family had been seen, she cried out, "Please don't shoot. We have done nothing. These are innocent children."

A Khmer Rouge ran to the ditch where we huddled.

My grandmother begged, "Take our gold and money. Please just leave us alone."

Then my uncle stood up. The Khmer Rouge demanded, "Where's the gun you bought last week?"

My uncle told him the truth, "I didn't buy any gun."

The Khmer Rouge raised his M-16 rifle and shot my uncle in the chest. Fired from that close range, the bullet careened through my uncle's body, and blood spewed out behind him. He fell dead on the ground.

My grandmother screamed. "Don't kill us," she begged. The killer sprayed her with bullets, and the rest of my family, too.

An M-16 bullet makes a small hole when it enters a human body. After it tears its way through the flesh, it exits, leaving a gaping hole the size of a fist.

I was shot three times. I lay limp in the ditch. It was filled with my family's blood. When a Khmer Rouge kicked my head one way, I let my head flop. He kicked it the opposite way, and I let it flop again. "If he knows I'm still alive," I thought, "he'll shoot me." Another Khmer Rouge kicked me again. They must have thought I was dead, so they didn't waste another bullet on me. A few minutes later, they were gone.

My youngest brother, barely five years old, was crying, and I tried to calm him. Hackly said nothing. He looked like he was in shock. My mother had held my little sister to her breast, hoping to keep her quiet as we squatted in the ditch. Now they were both silent. A single bullet pierced my little sister and then my mother's heart. With my right hand, I felt my baby sister's face. I found only a hole where her cheek should have been.

My mother was dead. My baby sister was dead. My grandmother was dead. My aunt and uncle were dead. My babysitter was dead.

I tried to get up, but my legs wouldn't work. I kept falling down into the bloody ditch. My left arm was so swollen I couldn't bend it. Two bullets had hit my elbow. Another had torn through my left hip.

My father heard the slaughter from his hiding place. Helpless, he stood in the dark, unable to see where to aim his gun or throw a grenade without killing us. He never told me what went through his mind that night. I never asked.

When the Khmer Rouge ran through the village, they had tossed grenades and burning matches at the houses. One of the grenades exploded inside a house near ours, killing all but one young boy, whose body was covered with shrapnel. Someone with a trailer behind his motorcycle took that boy and me to get medical help. Dad stayed at the scene of the massacre, trying to deal with the chaos that had just struck. On the way to the hospital, the boy next to me died.

My country is poor. At the hospital, there were no beds or good medicines. I lay on a piece of metal. The doctor told me, "You're lucky. If the bullet had hit an inch closer to your abdomen, your liver would have been destroyed."

I flinched when his assistant dabbed at the dried splotches of blood—my family's and my own—that covered me from my face to my feet. My arm hurt so much. I was scared, and I was alone. Then the doctor treated my bullet wounds. When he stitched them, with no painkiller, I cried, and then I screamed until I passed out.

The doctor later told me, "I did my best to put your smashed elbow back together. I made the cast hold your arm in a slightly bent position, so the elbow will set in a natural-looking angle. But I'm sorry, it will never flex normally again."

The bullet wounds slowly began to heal, but my misery was just beginning.

Chapter Two

FROM STUDENT TO SLAVE

I was born in Cambodia in 1964, the fifth of eight children. In those days, most families were big. My brothers and sisters and I were each about a year and a half apart. I had two older sisters, Chanya and Chantha, and two older brothers, Lee and Bunna (pronounced "BOOna"). My younger brothers were Hackly and Chanty, and our baby sister was Chantu. But we hardly ever used our formal names. Instead of calling me by my real name, Bunpah, everybody used my nickname "Mop" which meant "healthy baby."

My father was a successful rice farmer, one of the most prosperous in our little village of Salatrave. Most people lived in small, grass-roofed huts, but our two-story house was made of brick, and it had a tile roof. My father had built it on a large lot on the highest ground in the town. That location was important because it ensured that our house did not flood during the rainy season. We also had a tractor and a motorcycle, much more than other families owned. Our prosperity probably put us in extra danger from the Khmer Rouge. My father hired seasonal help during the rice harvest, and he also had one full-time worker who drove our tractor. That employee, named Zhen, often came to work drunk, and my father warned him he had to stop drinking. Zhen didn't change, so my father fired him. He ran away and joined the Khmer Rouge. With them, Zhen didn't have to worry about trying to make an honest living. Instead, he could get money by robbing and killing other people.

I do not know if Zhen encouraged the Khmer Rouge to target my family on that terrible night in 1973. But whether a family was singled out or not, no one was safe.

My older brothers and sister Chantha lived in the city of Battambang (BAHT-am-bong), and my oldest sister Chanya lived in the city of Pursat (Pa-SAHT). If they had been with us when the Khmer Rouge attacked, they might have been murdered too.

"Mop," my father said to me, "I'm going to send Hackly and Chanty to stay with Chantha where they will be safer."

"What about me?"

"I will take you to Pursat to live with Chanya. She can take care of you until your wounds heal. Then you can join Chantha and your little brothers in Battambang."

Cambodian children are very polite. I didn't question why he made his decisions. But I did ask, "Dad, what are you going to do?"

"I'll keep the farm going," he said.

I still couldn't understand what I had just experienced. It was too awful to be true. No matter how much my wounds hurt, my heart hurt even more.

How could my mother be dead? And my baby sister? My grandparents, too, and my uncle and aunt? It didn't seem real. And now my father was sending me away.

Chanya, her husband, and their baby welcomed me into their home in Pursat, which is about 10 miles (16 km) southeast of Salatrave, but I didn't feel happy to be there. I didn't feel happy about anything. But as the days and weeks passed, a routine developed. Thanks to Chanya's husband being a police officer, he had many professional friends. One of them was a doctor who came to the house to give me shots a couple of times a week to help prevent infection. He changed the dressing on my wounds and put my arm in a sling.

Chanya was kind to take me in, but she did not have my mother's sweet temperament. When we were kids all living at home, as the oldest one, she used to boss us younger kids around. Sometimes she spanked me. During the months I stayed with her in Pursat, she was very strict, and she yelled at me a lot. In the mornings, my gunshot wounds ached the most, but Chanya never let me stay in bed. If I said my arm hurt, she still made me get up early and drag myself to school.

I was glad when my wounds healed enough that I could go to Battambang. When my father picked me up from Chanya's, he said I was to help Chantha with my younger brothers. Chantha and I had always gotten along well. She was about four years older than I was, and she had a kind, gentle nature. She never complained or got mad. She was an excellent student, too.

I was already familiar with Battambang, which is about 12 miles (19 km) northwest of Salatrave. Before the Khmer Rouge came, I spent weekdays in Battambang going to school. That is because Salatrave was so small that it did not have a good school. Battambang was large, second in size only to the capital, Phnom Penh. After I finished kindergarten in Salatrave, my parents sent me to Battambang to study. My older brothers Lee and Bunna preferred to stay home and work on the farm, but my parents encouraged me to go to school. Chantha went, too. We lived in Battambang during the week with my uncle and his family. Every day I went to public elementary school. Then, after school let out in the late afternoon, I attended a private school for a couple of hours. I was allowed to go for free because the teacher was a friend of my father, and I was a good student. I saw kids who were not as fortunate as I hanging around the classroom door, eager to hear any wisdom the teacher might give. It was a privilege to be allowed a seat inside. The girls sat on one side of the classroom, the boys on the other. We were proud of our uniforms. We understood that education was important, and we worked hard. On Friday night, I would take the bus, which was like a small mini-van, back to Salatrave.

When the Khmer Rouge took over, everything changed. My uncle's family left Battambang, so my sister, Chantha, along with my brother Bunna, found a new place to live. Lee was staying by himself in Pursat.

When I moved in with Bunna and Chantha, Chantha tried to be a mother to my little brothers and me, but she was barely fifteen years old herself. She was busy with her own regular studies, and she spent a lot of time at her after-school classes. She was taking classes to help her prepare for a very hard exam that would determine whether she would be admitted to college. A smart man named Van Lan taught the prep classes. He was a few years older than Chantha, and he had been to college. Chantha liked studying with him.

I tried to concentrate on my schoolwork, but it was hard not to think about what had happened to my family. It made me especially sad to think of my mother, so I tried not to remember the terrible murders I'd witnessed. The best way to avoid the pain was to recite to myself, "Do not think about it. Do not think about it." But sometimes I couldn't help it. So when I thought about the past, I tried to focus on the good parts of our life before the Khmer Rouge came.

I remembered the fun of waiting for my mother's bus to come back to Salatrave from Battambang where she went for her weekly shopping trips. She always brought us candy and cookies. One time she brought me a special surprise—brand new plastic flip-flop sandals. I often went barefoot, so I was really excited. I loved those sandals.

We grew most of our own food, and my mother's weekly trips to Battambang supplied us with anything else we needed. But now and then my mother would send me to a house in the village to pick up something between her shopping trips. There were no stores. Everyone knew that certain items could be purchased from certain people, like pain pills from one family, or sugar or salt from others. If we wanted a snack, we could pick fruit from the trees. I especially liked guavas, which grew everywhere.

Every day my mother made us take a bath, but we didn't use bathtubs. Nobody had running water at home. If we needed fresh water, it had to be carried from the well in the center of town. We took a big clay pot with us. Because it is so hot in Cambodia, the water was always warm. To bathe, my friends or brothers and I took turns pouring pots full of water over each other. Because nobody had shampoo, we washed our hair just like we washed our body, under the spray of poured water. Chantha used clippers to trim my brothers' and my hair really close to our heads. We looked alike, bigger or smaller versions of each other depending on our ages.

We didn't have toilets, either. We used an outhouse. When I was little, I was always scared to go there by myself at night. Because there was no electricity, it was dark. Even though the outhouse was only 50 feet (15 m) away, the walk to it seemed much longer because in my imagination, giant monsters were hiding, waiting to get me.

We didn't always have to get the water from the well ourselves. My family could afford to hire teenagers to help us around the house. I was glad, because they did some of the chores, like getting the well water, washing clothes, sweeping the wooden floors in the house, and weeding our garden. In exchange for their work, my mom gave them food to take home to their families. Even with their help, my mom still had a lot of hard work to do. I remember her starting the cooking fire every day. She prepared the food over the flames, and the charcoal made our house really smoky. She was always rubbing her eyes, and mine stung, too.

Sometimes my mother would ask me to go with her to the rice field; "Mop, do you think you can walk all the way to the field with me? I want to re-seed a few sections."

"Yes, please, please, please!" I'd say.

What an adventure those special days were. For me, it was a rare treat to walk that far away from the house and to spend a whole day outside with my mother. I especially remember the fun I had on one of those trips during the rainy season. If I close my eyes, I can re-live the scene. I smelled the fresh moist air of the fields. The humidity made my skin feel extra soft. While Mom did the planting, I played in the mud nearby. I thought she would scold me for getting dirty, but she didn't. With my fingers and toes, I made patterns in the wet dirt. Then I collected rocks and arranged them in three piles, targets for clods of mud that I tossed at them. I backed farther and farther away, trying to improve my accuracy. Lots of times I flung the mud balls so hard that they fell apart even before they landed. When I hit the farthest target, I laughed. I'm good! When I felt too hot to stay in the sun any longer, I moved to the shade and wondered what to do. Then a bright green bird swooped in front of me. It was a bee-eater, a common sight in Salatrave. I wondered, "What would it be like to eat a bee? Wouldn't it sting you? And what would it be like to fly?" I pretended I could fly. I stretched out my arms and squawked at every bug I saw. Then I decided I'd eat some insects—but no bees—just to see what they tasted like. I caught a silver-colored insect with my hands, but its sparkly wings looked pretty and delicate. I didn't want to destroy them, so I opened my hand and let it go.

Mom said, "Mop, I'm done for the day. Let's walk back."

As we walked, I noticed tall wading birds in a rice field. They had red faces and long yellow legs. "What are those?," I asked.

"They're called lapwings," she said. "Some people say those birds sleep on their backs at night and stretch their long legs out straight to hold up the sky."

"Do you think that's true?" I asked.

"No," she said and laughed. "It's just a superstition."

"I don't believe it either," I said.

It seemed to me we walked a long ways. By the time we reached our house, I felt very worldly and important. When I got into bed that night, I raised my legs up toward the ceiling. I was glad I didn't have to do that all night long.

My mother was kind, but she made me behave, too. She scolded me when I got mad at my brothers. I hated their teasing me whenever our neighboor Deenah and her family stopped by to visit. I chased after them when they yelled, "Mop, here comes your wife!" Of course Deenah was not really my wife, but our marriage had been arranged. Nobody else in my family had an arranged marriage, but our mothers decided to arrange a marriage between Deenah and me because of a strange dream they each had. Just before Deenah and I were born, a couple that lived nearby passed away. Deenah's mother and my mother had an identical dream that the couple wanted to live with them. The mothers were so surprised by this that they decided their babies must have a special connection. This led to my mother's decision to name me "Bunpah." She thought the name seemed very grown-up, in anticipation of my marriage. I never liked that name because the last thing I wanted to think about was getting married. Like most kids, I wanted to think about playing and having fun. Deenah was nice, but I was too young to care about girls.

My older brother Bunna and I often got scolded for arguing. I remember one time I knew I was going to be in trouble. To get away from my mother, I scrambled up a coconut palm as high as I could go. My mother came looking for me, and when she saw me up there, she was scared I would fall down and be killed. She went away so that I would come down before I got so tired that I would fall out of the tree. When I came down unhurt she was so relieved that she did not even punish me.

My friends and I made up simple games. We played with rubber bands and marbles. Any piece of litter on the street could become a toy. We did not have organized teams or ball games. My good friend, Whee, lived next door. Sometimes he would come sleep over at my house, and sometimes I would go to his. We laughed a lot. He was older than me. In the Cambodian language, younger people usually speak more politely to older people. But we agreed to treat each other as equals. After the Khmer Rouge came, everything changed. I don't know what happened to Whee's family.

Now that I was living in Battambang with Chantha, I missed Salatrave, and especially my father. The Khmer Rouge had burned down most of our village, but every weekend I still liked to go there. Chantha and my brothers stayed in Battambang, and I took a taxi to see Dad. A taxi was a trailer pulled behind a motorcycle. The ride was scary, and even though Bunna was older than me, he was too timid to make the trip. I was scared, too, but I went anyway. I felt less nervous after my father arranged to have the same taxi take me each week. Even though the Khmer Rouge had blown up half of our house, Dad still lived there. He raised chickens, grew rice, and kept a big vegetable garden.

At the end of one of my visits to see Dad he said, "You're a good boy, Mop. Take this rice and these eggs, and vegetables. If there is any left over, tell Chantha to give the extra to anyone who needs it." Then he loaded the food next to me in the taxi trailer. As the taxi pulled away, I looked back and saw him standing alone in front of our ruined house. I tried to smile at him, but I couldn't.

He had told me I was a good boy. He usually did not talk much, and I was not accustomed to being praised. I wasn't sure if I was good or not. I was sure that I hated to leave him, but I had learned not to cry.

Back in Battambang, Chantha, my brothers, and I ate what Dad had supplied for us, and we shared it with the homeless children who begged on the streets. The Khmer Rouge had killed their parents and burned their houses, so many orphans in the city struggled to get enough to eat.

One weekend when I was at the farm with Dad, he said, "I have heard that the Khmer Rouge are gaining power. They are moving closer to the cities. Help me hitch the trailer to the tractor, and we'll drive it to Battambang."

As we rode along, my father said little. But I told him about Van Lan, who spent a lot of time with Chantha even when they weren't studying. He was starting to feel almost like a big brother to me, and a smart one at that. He had read a lot of books, and I liked hearing him talk.

I was used to riding in the tractor in Salatrave, but when we got to Battambang, it felt funny to be driving a farm vehicle into the city. People glanced at us, but no one stared. I think many of them wished they had any kind of transportation at all. We were lucky.

"Chantha and Bunna," Dad said, "if the Khmer Rouge come and you need to leave the city, load up as many of your belongings as you can fit into the trailer and return to Salatrave. You and your brothers can ride on the tractor."

Chantha looked down and then asked quietly, "What about Van Lan?"

My father said, "Chantha, what about Van Lan?"

"We want to get married," she said.

"I thought so," he said. "Of course you should all be safe together."

Chantha smiled slightly. This was not the way an engagement announcement was supposed to be made. Like most Cambodian girls, she had always looked forward to planning her wedding with the help of our mom, and savoring her beautiful day as a bride. As for my arranged marriage to Deenah, that idea was a thing of the past. Most of her family had been killed by the Khmer Rouge. Deenah survived, but I had no idea where she was. After the Khmer Rouge came, sorrow and uncertainty had taken over our lives. Our world had fallen apart, and we didn't know what our new world would be like.

"Thank you for understanding," she said to Dad.

Dad left the tractor and trailer with us, and he took a taxi back to the farm. Soon his prediction proved true.

We heard rumors that Pol Pot, the leader of the Khmer Rouge, thought city folk were too privileged and couldn't be trusted. Pol Pot said farming was the only right way for everyone to live. In 1975 the Khmer Rouge streamed into Battambang and Phnom Penh. They didn't talk about their philosophy. Instead, at gunpoint, they yelled, "Get out of here, or we'll shoot! Now!" They were deadly serious. We could hear gunshots, and terrified children screaming. Van Lan said, "Mop, help me carry all the bags of rice that we have. Then choose any clothes you want to take."

Chantha said, "I'll get our clothes and help Hackly and Chanty with theirs."

Van Lan said calmly, "We can do this. Bring everything to the tractor, and I'll load it all up."

Van Lan and I each carried two bags of rice out to the tractor. At age ten, I still wasn't very strong, but fear gives you muscle power you didn't know you had. The street was jammed with people lugging as much as they could manage on their backs and in their arms. A few had bicycles or taxis, but most people walked. I heard a little girl cry, "Mommy, where are we going?" I ran back into the house and grabbed a couple of shirts, a pair of shorts, and my pajamas. I put them in a sack and took them to Van Lan. Chantha brought out a larger sack, and Hackly and Chanty, looking scared, trailed behind her. Van Lan organized everything in the tractor, and we piled in.

We had it easier than most people, because we had transportation. When we recognized other families going to Salatrave, we added their belongings to ours on the tractor, and they walked alongside. We were all nervous. I was glad Van Lan was with us. He spoke slowly and acted confident in spite of the chaos in the street. He was barely 20 years old, but to me, he seemed like an adult.

The Khmer Rouge walked in the streets, yelling and waving their guns. "Thanks to our great leader Pol Pot, we have a new Cambodia! Call us 'Angka.' " "Angka" meant "savior," but we needed saving from these hoodlums.

"City ways are evil," yelled another Khmer Rouge. "In the new Cambodia, everyone works for the common good. They don't sit around in fancy offices. They grow rice. If you don't like the new way, then you are the enemy. The enemy will not live!"

While throngs of people trudged out of the city, the Khmer Rouge started killing "the enemy." They shot educated people, advanced students, civic and military leaders, old people, and anyone with money. The Khmer Rouge had no laws. There were no courts. If they did not like somebody, they killed him. If a bystander complained, he got shot too. We watched in horror, silently. Fortunately, the Khmer Rouge did not know Van Lan was a teacher. They simply did not notice him. We got out of the city safely, but we had no idea what awaited us.

We returned to our village, Salatrave. But nobody was allowed to move into their old houses, or what was left of them. We had to build huts made of leaves, grass, and poles. Each family had a hut. The Khmer Rouge made us build them side by side, in long rows. Ours was at the end.

One day right after we got to Salatrave, my father said, "Chantha and Van Lan, you should have a beautiful wedding, full of celebration and joy. But it's obvious that is not possible in these times."

"I want to marry your daughter properly," said Van Lan.

"I know," said Dad, "that's what we all want. I have a

friend who can perform the ceremony. I'll invite whatever family is able to come."

The ceremony was simple and short. In our village, people usually celebrated a wedding by playing music on a battery-powered record player with a speaker so large that everyone in town could enjoy the music. Someone still had one of those players, and after the ceremony, hearing the traditional music made me feel good. Chantha and Van Lan grinned, and I did too.

"Mop, I am now your brother," said Van Lan with a wink. That gave me the biggest reason to smile that I'd had in a long time. But I could tell the grown-ups were not as happy as you would expect at a wedding. We didn't know what the future would bring.

Only a few days later, the Khmer Rouge brought their guns again and yelled, "Move, now!"

They made all of us leave the huts we had just built. In the next weeks, a pattern developed. Over and over again, they forced us to work in a field for a few days, and then set up a camp nearby to sleep in. Then they would make us move to another area and do the same thing again. I never asked why. I just did what I was told.

My father heard that the Khmer Rouge near Salatrave did not like him, and he understood what that meant— his murder. So he left us and hid in the jungle where the trees, shrubs, and vines grew so close together that it was easy to become lost. But he was really smart, and he quickly learned his way around. He brought two friends to the area where he was living, and together they fished and gathered honey at beehives he had found. Then the men took the fish and honey to people in Salatrave. Some of the Khmer Rouge were glad to have the food added to their supplies, so they accepted what my father's friends brought them, and they did not go after my father in the jungle. I missed him so much!

The Khmer Rouge made us work in the fields every day. We did not get paid, and there were no days off. I had never worked in the fields before, but I did what the Khmer Rouge told me to do. I was just a kid, but that didn't matter. I was a slave.

Everybody in Cambodia, even people who had never been farmers, knew that rice grows in shallow water. We built levees to keep the fields flooded. Sometimes we weeded the rice paddies. We made fertilizer out of tree bark and spread it in the fields. The other kids and I scared away birds that tried to eat the rice. At the end of the day, the Khmer Rouge made us set up our sleeping shacks.

One day when I was working in a rice field, I saw Zhen, the drunken employee my father had fired. Now, like the other Khmer Rouge men, he wore black. I pretended not to see him. When he got really close to me, he said in a mean voice, "Where is your father?"

"I don't know," I said.

"Yes you do," he said. "Tell me." He grabbed my arm and yanked me closer to him.

"I don't know. I really don't." I looked down, the polite way for children to talk with adults.

"I'll find him, you nasty brat," he said. He shoved me away and strode off, sneering at us in the field.

Before the Khmer Rouge took over, he never would have been so mean to me. He worked for my father and was courteous to my whole family. Now Zhen was the boss with his rifle, black clothes, and show-off swagger.

Once when the Khmer Rouge made us walk to new fields, we marched past our old village. We saw that our house and all our neighbors' houses had been flattened. Even if the Khmer Rouge decided to let us go home, I saw that I no longer had a home to go to.

After my father left for the jungle, the rest of my family still stayed together—Bunna, Chantha, Van Lan, my younger brothers and I. Lee was still living by himself in Pursat, and Chanya was still there, too, with her family. We cooked and ate our own food, away from other people. That arrangement lasted for only a few months. Then the Khmer Rouge took our little grill, cooking supplies, and food away from us. We were ordered to eat one meal a day with the group, but there was not enough food to go around. The Khmer Rouge said, "Now there may not be much food, but in the future there will be. If you work hard enough, you will have three full meals a day."

To have three full meals a day became my dream.

When people do not have enough to eat, they get weak, they get sick, and they die. A lot of people died. We did not know what was going to happen to us. Would we be strong enough to survive? Would the Khmer Rouge decide to shoot us? Would our lives ever return to normal, or would we always be slaves who did nothing but grow rice, and hope for almost enough food to eat in return for our endless labor?

At night when I tried to fall asleep, my stomach growled with hunger. I tried to remember what it was like to have plenty to eat. I thought about the Cambodian Thanksgiving when Mom prepared delicious, traditional food that I loved. I could picture her soaking the rice in water overnight. Then she put bacon or bananas on it, and wrapped it all in a banana leaf. The next day, she boiled it for a long time, until it cooked through. Sometimes we ate it with a fork, and sometimes we just peeled back the banana leaf and ate it with our hands. We did not have electricity or a refrigerator (nobody did), so we did not store food for long. I loved these rice pockets, and sometimes I hid some, hoping to save them for later. But the bugs, rats, or birds would always eat the food before I got back to it. How I wished I had that food now.

Cambodians do not celebrate birthdays, but we do love holidays, and food is always part of them. At our New Year's celebration, the family always got together for a big meal. I especially liked the fruit we would have for the party. It came from other regions of Cambodia, so we did not normally eat it. But for New Year's we would splurge and buy it. To get to the reunion, some relatives from far away came on motorcycles. Others came in taxis. People who lived fairly close came by cyclo, a kind of sofa on a bicycle. On the back, a man pedals a bicycle, and the "sofa" sits on his handlebars, which are supported by two wheels. I was scared whenever I rode in a cyclo, because if the rider ran into anything, I—sitting in front—would have been the human bumper! But now, we never rode in any vehicle at all. We just walked and worked. The Khmer Rouge even took our clothes. They left me with only one pair of shorts and a shirt, which soon became nothing but rags.

During the rainy season, the Khmer Rouge sent my brother Bunna, then 15 years old, far away to work with a *chalat* (zhaLOT). It was a group of boys and girls about his age or a few years older that would make small earthen dams for irrigation or build huts for the Khmer Rouge. They worked on each project for three or four months at a time, all day long. Like the other teenagers with him, Bunna always longed for his family. One time he ran away to see us. He traveled by day through the jungle. He stayed away from the main trails or roads where he might be seen. He crawled through the murky marshes where almost nobody went during the rainy season. He also traveled by night. He knew that if the Khmer Rouge saw him, they would not bother to ask questions. They would consider him the enemy, and probably shoot him.

But one night, he just appeared!

"What are you doing here?" we asked in amazement.

"Shh!" he whispered. "I'm hungry. I haven't had enough to eat since I left the chalat four days ago." It was wonderful to have him back, but we were scared all the time. So was he. His talent was in drawing and painting, not doing brave deeds. Usually a timid person, he did not like to take chances. He hid in the jungle during the day while we worked in the rice fields, but after we got back and it was dark, he would join us. We had no lights except for small gas lamps, so no one could see him.

We did not ask Bunna to tell stories about what his life was like in the chalat. He did not ask about our work in the rice fields. All we had was the family—or what was left of us—being together. We managed to stay alive, day after day, but we had no hopes or dreams for the future. We had no freedom to control the present, much less next month or next year. We did not know if the rest of our lives would be like this—nothing but work, hunger, and fear, just waiting until we died. Sadness takes away your energy, your laughter, and your love of life. All we had was love for our family, and that's what made us want to survive.

After a few weeks, Bunna came to us and said, "I know this good luck cannot last forever. It's not safe for me to stay here with you." He was worried about what would happen if he were found with us when he was supposed to be with the chalat. Would the Khmer Rouge shoot us all? After a few weeks, he sneaked back up to the work camp he had fled.

My father, still hiding out in the jungle, was desperate to see any of his children. My younger brothers were not strong enough to walk a long way, but I was. I think Dad asked his two friends who worked for him to get permission from the local Khmer Rouge boss to let them bring me with them. Maybe the Khmer Rouge were so glad to get the extra food supplied by my father that they didn't mind if I, just one little kid, was away from the fields for a while. I don't know what the Khmer Rouge thought. For me it was simple: I liked to be with Dad, and if the Khmer Rouge would let me join him, I would go.

Chapter Three

THE JUNGLE

Dad rarely spoke. Instead, he showed me things.

He showed me how to catch wild chickens in the jungle, and any other birds we could get. We used fishing line. It was hard to find, and we used only as much as we needed to trap the birds. To make the trap, we laid a branch across a trail. We trimmed its leaves so that wandering chickens would notice only one easy route to follow as they walked along pecking for food on the ground. When they were channeled into the narrow spot we selected, they would step into a noose we had made. The string tightened around their feet, and at that moment, the tree branch we tied it to would swing up, pulling the bird with it. Every day I checked the traps. How I loved it when we had snared a bird!

Dad was a genius at finding turtle eggs. I would search and search for them, and then I'd say, "None here." Dad would shake his head, point to soft ground, dig a tiny bit, and pull up a handful of eggs. They were the most delicious food we had in the jungle.

He also showed me how to make popcorn. He dug a small hole and made a fire in it. The fire heated the dirt until it hardened. Then he put corn into the hole, and it popped, one kernel at a time. We caught each popping kernel. It was so much fun.

I spent many months with Dad in the jungle. We stayed in an abandoned hut next to a small pond. We ate fish from the pond, but Dad thought the water was not safe to drink, so we boiled it first. We lived so deep in the jungle, only his two helpers knew where we were. We saw nobody else.

In the morning, the birds made our only company. I loved to watch the colorful bee-eaters sail through the air, darting and swooping as they grabbed bees, wasps, and other insects. Larger birds soared gracefully above the pond and then dove down to grab fish for their breakfast. Woodpeckers high in the trees tapped the trunks in their search for insects. I could hear the calls of birds that I could not see because of the dense jungle. Their beautiful songs welcomed each dawn. I agreed with them that dawn was worth welcoming. Instead of the terrible sadness I felt when I slaved in the rice fields every day, I liked being with my father in a place that seemed far away from the Khmer Rouge.

Even though we spent all our time there together, Dad never told me any stories about my mother or about his life before the Khmer Rouge came. I will never know the reason. Maybe he thought I was too young to understand. He might have been too miserable himself to be able to talk with me about all that he had lost. He sat quietly and smoked cigarettes. Cambodian children are very respectful toward their parents. I understood that I should not ask him "why?"

Even though we seldom spoke, my mind was always working. I imagined us back at home, enjoying our normal life before the Khmer Rouge came. Dad was a kind, gentle person. He never yelled at me or spanked me. I remember him showing me his collection of antique rifles. I loved to stare at them and picture him using them. He told me that when he was a boy, one of his jobs was to herd cattle and to protect them from lions and other animals that used to be in the jungle. He carried a gun then, but the gun couldn't protect him from everything. One day a wild boar attacked him, and on his leg he still had the scar made by the boar's tusk. On the wall of our house, he displayed the stuffed head of a wild boar he had killed.

Dad told me the biggest rifle in his collection was an elephant gun. It was huge! He did not use it to shoot elephants. Instead, he aimed it toward the sky. The loud noise would scare the elephants away. I smiled at the memory of how I used that gun once, but not to scare an elephant. Most of the kids in my village were my friends, but a few were jealous of our family because we were the richest in town. One time some bullies threw rocks at my younger brother and me. We were so mad, we ran to the house and took my Dad's old elephant gun down from the wall. We knew it did not work anymore, but we carried it outside so the bullies could see it. Boy, did we laugh when they ran away, dropping their stones as they went. We felt as strong as elephants that day!

In the summer in Cambodia, it does not rain at all. Everything dries out, and the dirt cakes to a hard, cracked surface. The opposite happens in the winter. Then, there is too much water. When I was a little boy in Salatrave, I liked the flooding. My family's house was on high ground, so it never got wet. But across the road, some of the backyards flooded. The other kids and I waded in the water that made the familiar yards seem like strange lagoons. We pointed at fish swimming in ditches where only a few weeks before we had played hide-and-seek. We laughed to see fish swimming above low tree branches where we hung out on lazy afternoons in the dry season.

Now, living in the jungle, I didn't consider flooding to be a source of fun. Because the water covered almost everything, we could not find turtle eggs. It covered the grass and came up above our knees. To fish, we stretched a very thin vine just above the water's surface. Every few feet, we hung fishhooks from it, baited with worms or little frogs. After a couple of hours, we left the higher ground where the hut stood, and we waded through the water to see if we had had any luck. The line sagged a little bit if a fish had been caught. We could tell if we had caught a snake or eel because they made a whirlpool from swirling around in the flooded grasses. We ate whatever we caught.

Dad showed me how to make a monkey trap. Using the only tool he had, his machete, he cut a branch into four pieces, each about two feet long. He whittled the end of each one into a point. We pushed those into the ground to be the four corners of our trap. Then we twisted vines and sticks together to be the walls and top of our primitive cage. It had a little door that we pulled open with a vine attached to a twig we lay at an angle on the bottom of the trap. One end of the twig was on the ground, but the other end was lifted about an inch by the vine tied to the trap door. We baited the trap with a few grains of rice. We hoped that a monkey would climb through the door to get the rice. Then, when the monkey stepped on the twig held up by the vine, the vine would slip off the end of the twig, and the door would close with the monkey caught inside.

We set three traps, each one on a different trail, not far from our camp. The jungle is so thick, nobody can walk through it unless there's a trail.

The first time I trapped a monkey, I was scared. I yelled for Dad to come. My yelling scared the monkey, too. He panicked and managed to squeeze between the sticks and scramble out of the trap. My father said to me, "Next time you find a trapped monkey, you have to be silent. You have to be brave. Can you do that?"

I looked down, ashamed of myself for letting the monkey get away. "I can do it," I said, but I wasn't sure if I really could.

The next time we trapped a monkey, I did not yell. I just ran to tell Dad. He came and showed me how to grab the monkey without letting it bite me. I learned how to tie the monkey up and take it back to our camp. But I always felt scared of monkeys, because some of them are really big, and they're very smart. I carried a knife to protect myself.

Before the Khmer Rouge took over, our family always ate normal food like beef, chicken, and fish. But in the jungle during the rainy season, we had the choice of starving to death, or eating any food that was available. Monkey meat could keep us alive. Eating monkeys was disgusting. But if we did not eat them, we would die.

Besides the monkeys, we lived on crickets, rats, snakes, and frogs. I killed snakes by beating on them with a stick. The water snakes were not poisonous, but many of the ones on land were, like the cobra. But the most deadly was the one we called an inside-out snake. We gave it that name because of its coloring. Its back had a simple pattern of black scales, and its belly had the same pattern, in reverse, of white scales. One bite would kill a person.

In Cambodia, we believe that a snake that sees a pregnant woman cannot move. Only its head can move. A few years before, I saw a pregnant woman I knew step on an inside-out snake. The snake moved its head just enough to bite her. When I saw the snake, I recognized what kind it was. It was too late to help the woman. She turned blue and died.

In the jungle, I did not spend much time worrying about poisonous snakes. The Khmer Rouge seemed far more dangerous to me. I think Dad felt the same. When the dry season came, he sent me out of the jungle. I will never know for sure, but I think he was afraid the Khmer Rouge were going to come after him, and he wanted me to be safe.

I left with his two workers. I walked out of the jungle carrying a long stick on my shoulder. At both ends, I had tied big turtles we had caught. Cambodians love to eat turtle meat, so I had a valuable contribution to give the people. Maybe my father thought that if the Khmer Rouge liked the turtle meat, they would be nice to me. But one of the turtles, swinging as I walked, stretched its neck and bit my arm. Cambodians have a saying that if a turtle bites you, it will not let go until it hears thunder. "Oh, no!" I screamed. It was the dry season. Would that turtle hold onto my arm all summer until the thunder came? I was so scared, I flung the pole down to the ground as hard as I could. The force of my throw made the turtle let go of my arm. I breathed a sigh of relief and rubbed my sore arm. Then I picked up the pole again. Both turtles were still tied on. After that, I walked more carefully so they did not swing close to me. I stayed safe from the turtles, but other dangers awaited me.

Chapter Four

JAIL WITHOUT WALLS

"Nothing has changed," said Van Lan when I rejoined him, Chantha, and my younger brothers. The Khmer Rouge made them work in the rice fields from sunup to sundown, seven days a week. Once again, I had to do the same. There was no such thing as a holiday or a day off. We had no games, no toys, no fun. We barely had enough food. We were not even allowed to eat the very same rice that we grew. Anyone caught "stealing" rice was "the enemy."

The Khmer Rouge destroyed all the motorcycles, trucks, cars, and even tractors. Everyone lived in temporary shacks, and at gunpoint the Khmer Rouge herded people from field to field to clear land or harvest rice. The guards constantly changed, so no friendships developed between them and us. The Khmer Rouge had families, but I kept away from them. They got all the food, and if I went near any of their food, the guards might have said I was trying to steal it. It was safest to never have anything to do with Khmer Rouge families. They looked different from us only because they were not skinny and hungry. The men wore black clothes and always carried guns.

I would have run away if there had been a place to go. Anyone found off by himself was suspected of being a runaway. He would probably be shot, and as punishment, his family would be killed, too. Cambodians really love their families, and they don't want to risk their family's lives. Anyone who complained would be shot or beaten to death with a hammer or hoe. The Khmer Rouge were known to kill anyone who had a scar from a bullet. They figured that if the person had been shot before, then that person must have been the enemy. I did my best to hide the scars from my bullet wounds, but I think the Khmer Rouge didn't pay much attention to me. As far as they were concerned, I was just an unimportant kid.

Almost all handicapped people were killed. It didn't matter to the Khmer Rouge why somebody was disabled. Maybe they'd been hurt on their farm, or maybe a Khmer Rouge grenade had hit them. The Khmer Rouge would look at a handicapped person and say, "You're the enemy." That meant he would have to die. The Khmer Rouge gave people no opportunity for an explanation. One day I heard a Khmer Rouge yell at a man standing awkwardly in a rice field. "Straighten up and get to work, you lazy old man!" he yelled.

The man slowly lifted his shoulders, but he stood unevenly.

"You can't work," said the Khmer Rouge. "What good are you?"

"I am a man, that is all," he answered with his head bowed.

"In a bowl of rice, nobody misses one grain. Nobody will miss you. Come with me," said the Khmer Rouge.

"I have a wife and two children," he said quietly. "They need me."

The Khmer Rouge screamed at him, "Nobody needs you. Get going!" He pointed his gun toward the edge of the field. The man limped in front of him, with the Khmer Rouge shoving and pushing from behind. After they went into the dense forest and I couldn't see them any more, I heard a gun shot. The Khmer Rouge came back alone.

There was no justice.

The Khmer Rouge killed anybody who seemed especially smart. I was smart enough to keep quiet.

People who did not know how to get food on their own starved to death if they depended only on the small amount of food the Khmer Rouge allowed us to have. One such group of people were the Chinese living in Cambodia. Although there were not many, most of them ran businesses in the cities. When the Khmer Rouge kicked everybody out of the cities, the Chinese had no idea how to survive in the country. Almost all of them died. Whenever I could, I caught crabs and gave them to the Chinese people.

I had no sense of a future that might be different from the present. Nobody did. Our existence was so awful, some people did not want to live. They felt no hope, and they committed suicide.

I wanted to live because of my family. We no longer had a mother, and our father was away. We had only ourselves, and we had to take care of each other. Every morning when I woke up and saw the faces of Chantha and Van Lan, and my younger brothers, Hackly and Chanty, I said to myself, "This family is all I have. I am lucky to be alive."

One afternoon a Khmer Rouge boss walked up to my sister. He told Chantha, "Take this two-wheeled cart. This pair of cattle will pull it. You and your family can return to your village."

I was full of questions, but I knew not to ask.

In the morning, my younger brothers and I got in the cart, and Chantha and Van Lan walked alongside. We started off for Salatrave. My heart pounded. For once, I was not working in the rice fields. I was just sitting in a cart, and we were traveling a familiar road toward my home. We recognized another family from our village who also had a cart loaded up with their children. "So two families were going. Were the Khmer Rouge going to let people return to their old way of living?" I wondered. That seemed too good to be true, but I hoped it would be true. I kept my mouth shut, but my eyes wide open.

On the way to Salatrave, we passed through several villages. In one of them, Van Lan knew someone. He had been his adopted brother. In Cambodia, if a child was orphaned, it was common for a generous family to take him in until he grew up. This man had lived with Van Lan's family. He invited us to have a meal and stay overnight with him. In fact, he warned Van Lan that we would be foolish to continue to Salatrave that day. Van Lan listened carefully.

Van Lan told Chantha, "Let's stay here tonight. If the Khmer Rouge ask why we didn't travel straight through, I will say 'the cart's wheel is broken,' or 'one of the cattle started limping.' " So we stopped. The other family continued on the road. When we got to Salatrave the next day, people there greeted us with surprise. They told us the other family had been killed in an ambush.

No official organization ruled the Khmer Rouge, but I guess the local leader had been told by another leader to kill two families traveling with their children in carts that day. Van Lan's foster brother knew about this plot. The Khmer Rouge killed the only family they saw, and then they left the area. I suppose the Khmer Rouge who wanted us to be killed did not find out we survived. Why did the Khmer Rouge want to destroy my family? Maybe Zhen, the worker we fired, had tried to set it up. I will never know.

For a few months, we stayed together in Salatrave and worked for the Khmer Rouge there. But then they sent my younger brothers and me away to live and work with other children. We felt so lonely without Chantha and Van Lan. I tried to set a brave example for them, but I was still young, too. As usual during the rainy season, the Khmer Rouge slept on the high ground so they could stay dry and comfortable. In the area where we were working, there was only one other high spot. It was the site of a Buddhist temple, now partly destroyed. The

Khmer Rouge boss yelled at me, "You and your brothers will sleep next to the temple. Over there. Go!"

I was horrified to step onto that ground because that's where cremations occurred. Human bones and ashes covered the soil. We walked really slowly, and the Khmer Rouge yelled again, "Hurry up, you spoiled kids. I'm not going to wait around here forever while you take your own sweet time."

I knew we had no choice. We lay down on our backs, side by side. I made sure not to look around much because it's hard to fall asleep when skulls are staring at you. My brothers were really scared. I told them, "There's an old story that lapwings, those tall wading birds, have a special way of sleeping."

"What is it?" asked Hackly.

"They lie on their backs and stick their legs straight up. It's important that they do that."

"Why?"

"People say that their legs hold the sky up all night long. The sky hasn't fallen, so they must be nearby, keeping us safe. Let's dream about lapwings."

When we were moved to work in other fields, there was even less high, dry ground. The Khmer Rouge slept there, and they made us sleep where everything was wet. Tender skin develops a rash when it is exposed to water every day and every night, never having a chance to dry. My thighs and shins turned red, and the skin felt as if it was burning up. We didn't have towels, cream, or anything that could help. If I touched my legs, the skin seemed to burn even more. There was no relief until the wet season ended.

The Khmer Rouge never let us stay in one spot for long. We had no place that felt like a home. Every now and then we were moved to fields near where Chantha and Van Lan were working. We stayed together at night, sleeping in small huts we made of tall grass. It felt good to be with my family—we were all we had. Everybody's huts were close together, so it was impossible for us to have a private conversation. Two old men talked late one night about how they could resist the Khmer Rouge. Somebody overheard them. The next day, they were taken away from the camp. They were killed. After that, nobody dared to talk about anything with anybody. We kept quiet and tried not to be noticed. We avoided talking about our past because if a Khmer Rouge overheard us and happened to know and dislike one of our old friends, he might decide he didn't like us, either. I did not try to make friends with other boys my age. What if one of them, for whatever reason, said something bad about me to the Khmer Rouge?

I could barely remember when I used to play games with my friends, laughing at fish swimming in flooded back yards, running just for the fun of it, or joking with my schoolmates. My old childhood seemed to be part of another life—someone else's, not mine.

Chapter Five

HUNGER

"**We have to stretch** the rice as much as we can. Let's boil these grains," said Chantha. "We'll make rice soup." She poured a few grains into the water, and let it simmer.

We drank the broth, but there wasn't much nutrition. It was rice-flavored water. We still felt hungry. It was the rainy season in 1976, and food had become even scarcer.

"Mop, see if any chaff is left in the bag. Some residue from the rice might still cling to it," said Van Lan.

I scooped out a handful of the chaff, the part people normally don't eat. We tried it. The chaff was so small that it caught in our digestive tracts. During the night, we woke up with cramps in our gut. The chaff was not edible, and we had nothing else to eat.

That year, more people died of starvation than from bullets. Most days when I left the rice fields and went to the group shack for my one meal of the day, I was told, "The food is all gone." Instead of having a dream of three meals a day, my dream was reduced to having just one meal a day.

Some of the grown-ups said the Khmer Rouge traded a lot of the rice to China in exchange for guns and ammunition. Some said they sold rice on the black market to Vietnam, the country east of Cambodia, and then used the money to buy American guns. I didn't know what the truth was. All I understood was that for the first time in my life, I was always hungry.

Before the Khmer Rouge took over, I ate well. Even the poorest people had enough food. But after the Khmer Rouge gained power, everybody was hungry. If we saw a snake in the water of the rice paddies, it didn't live long. We ate it.

The Khmer Rouge caught one old woman taking rice for her family. The guards tied her on a mound covered with big red ants. The ants crawled all over her face and body. She screamed all day long as they bit her everywhere. No one could help her. If they did, they'd suffer the same torture or worse.

When I woke up one morning, Van Lan was gone. When the other families were getting up and making some noise, Chantha whispered to me, "Van Lan has gone to see his parents. Don't worry, he'll come back."

No matter what she said, she looked worried. My eyes opened wide in fear. What would happen to us without him?

Chantha whispered again, "He has a friend in the Khmer Rouge. Van Lan promised that he'll bring him something good if he lets Van Lan go away for a few days."

I couldn't believe it. Van Lan was friends with a Khmer Rouge?

"Van Lan knows how to be safe. I am sure he'll come back okay."

With Van Lan gone, I felt even more scared, and even more responsible for my brothers and sister.

For several months I had been working in the vegetable garden that was supposed to provide food for us children. But the Khmer Rouge took the best for themselves. Once a day they gave us a bowl of watered down vegetable stew. It wasn't enough. In the evening, I asked the Khmer Rouge to give us rice chaff to use for fertilizer. Because people cannot eat the chaff, the Khmer Rouge would not think it was important to keep. I brought another kid who worked in the garden with me to the rice storage barn. There was no electricity, so the building was dark. After I took the sacks they gave me for the chaff, I noticed piles of rice in the corner. When the Khmer Rouge were paying attention to the other kid, I quickly stuffed fistfuls of rice into the bottom of my sacks. When I left the building, the guards only glanced at the top of the bags and didn't discover my trick. We had enough food for the next few days.

The Khmer Rouge had guns, they had food, they had everything. But I still had my brain and the courage to use it. One trick I learned was to sneak to the vegetable garden and pick squash when no one else was around. If I was caught carrying it back to our shack, I might be shot for stealing food. So, I didn't carry it. I tied one end of a long vine around my knee and the other around the squash. Then, I dragged the squash along. Whenever I stopped, the vine drooped, and the squash stayed far enough behind me that nobody could see I was pulling it.

In the swamps next to the fields, I watched fish and eels glide into snake and crab holes, and then I reached into the holes and grabbed them. Sometimes I made fish traps out of bamboo. I arranged the sticks into a loose bundle that was narrow at one end, wide at the other. Fish would swim into the wide end and not be able to figure out how to find their way back out. The next morning when it was still dark, I'd get up early to check my traps. I hid the fish I caught inside my waistband so that the Khmer Rouge would not see what I had.

After I got a fish back to our shack, it was hard to hide, because it would get smelly and go bad. We needed salt to preserve it, but salt was rare and precious. If anybody had salt, they hid it as carefully as they hid gold jewelry. I believed salt was more valuable than jewelry. Gold might be worth money, but what was there to buy? Besides, you can't eat gold. People who ate nothing but fish and rice died from malnutrition. In a tropical jungle climate, people need salt.

My youngest brother, Chanty, had a bloated belly and constant diarrhea, signs of malnutrition. One day when I returned from the field, I discovered that he had eaten most of a raw fish that my family had been saving. We were trying to stretch the food over time. But he was so hungry, and he was so small, he simply ate it. We could not blame him.

About a week after Van Lan left, I woke up to see a wonderful sight. He was back! What a relief. I don't know what he gave to the Khmer Rouge, but I saw what he brought us—fresh oranges. These were treasures. My brothers and I each ate one, as slowly as we could make ourselves, in order to extend the pleasure. We savored the sweetness, inhaled the fresh aroma, and our tongues explored the texture of each orange section. We licked the inside and the outside of the peel to get every bit of taste. We would have more of them that night, and the next morning, too. I remembered before the Khmer Rouge came when I used to pick fruit from a tree whenever I wanted a snack. In those days, I didn't think twice about it. Now, these precious oranges helped keep us alive. My sister especially needed the food, because she was pregnant. She and Van Lan did not talk with excitement about the baby that was on the way. Instead, everyone focused on getting enough to eat.

The Khmer Rouge said we could not have any of the rice from the fields we worked in. "That would be stealing!" they said. "We kill thieves." But we saw people die from starvation, so we "stole" rice whenever we could.

Late one evening, Van Lan said, "Mop, will you help me get some rice?"

"Of course, but how?" I said.

"Rice is ready to harvest in a field I saw about a mile

north of here. If we wait until dark, we might be able to snatch a bag full."

"OK, I'm ready," I said as bravely as I could.

When we got to the field, Van Lan walked ahead of me. I stayed close behind him because it was hard to see in the darkness. The birds were quiet, and we did not speak. We moved slowly, looking around to be sure we were alone.

"Hey, you!" A man's voice rang out, angry and loud. A Khmer Rouge was guarding the field, and he had heard us. He yelled again, and another guard joined him. They ran toward us.

Van Lan and I took off as fast as we could. We got separated. I tried to hide in a termite mound. My foot sank down and I felt something hard. I'd stepped into a shallow human grave. A bone with smelly, rotting human flesh clung to my bare foot. I made myself hold still, and the guards didn't see me. They ran past me and chased Van Lan.

My heart pounded. What should I do? Where was Van Lan? Did the Khmer Rouge catch him? If they did, I stopped myself from thinking about what could happen next.

I listened as hard as I could. When it was quiet, I sneaked away. I decided not to walk on the road, because if the Khmer Rouge came back, they would easily see me there. So, I crouched low and walked off the road in the flooded jungle. I sloshed through the water, stopping every few seconds to listen.

After what felt like hours of terrified wading, I made it back to our family's shack. There was Van Lan! We had both been lucky. With relief, I collapsed into a deep sleep. In the morning, I tore off a huge, engorged leech that clung to my leg.

Most days the Khmer Rouge let us each have a handful of rice, but that was not enough to live on. When I was hungry, my body craved food so much that I could not relax and sleep. But what good was food if I could not cook it and make it edible? The Khmer Rouge had taken all our cooking utensils. So, I used all I had—a thin rag that the Khmer Rouge had not bothered to confiscate. I put the handful of rice in it. Then I dug a small hole and buried the little rice-filled sack in the ground. In the evening, I started a small fire on the ground above it. If any Khmer Rouge questioned me, I could say I made the fire just to watch it burn. There was nothing else around. The rice, buried in the dirt below, cooked from the heat of the fire. How did I learn this trick? I simply thought of it. The alternative was starvation, and I wanted to live.

Like everybody else, if I had a tiny bit of food, I ate it. There were no family meals together. Even if there had been enough food for all of us to eat as a family, the Khmer Rouge would have thought that our having so much food would be proof that it was "stolen." They shot thieves.

Chantha's belly never bulged out big like the healthy pregnant women I used to see, but the baby grew, and she finally gave birth. She had a healthy boy, and they named him Vibol. No one felt much joy about bringing a child into that terrible life.

One night when Van Lan was sent away to harvest a distant crop, Chantha asked me to sneak over to a rice field and grab some rice for her so she could have the strength to feed the baby. My brothers and I were hungry, too.

Carrying a pillowcase to gather the rice, I sneaked out. My brother Chanty said, "I want to come along." I let him, but I should have known better.

A Khmer Rouge spotted us as we neared the rice field. Chanty hid in a termite mound. I ran and ran through the darkness and the flooded fields. Then I was jolted to a painful halt. My foot had sunk into a knee-deep hole. My leg almost broke. A Khmer Rouge jumped on me, put his foot on my neck, and held me under the water. I thought I was going to drown, but then he pulled me up. I gasped for air, he yelled at me, and pushed me under again. I knew I was being killed. It was all over.

He and his buddies kicked me in the legs. Using their fists, they punched my stomach, arms and head. When they got sick of beating me up, they tied my hands behind my back, and told me to call my brother. I did, and he came.

The gang marched us hour after hour to another town. Chanty and I did not dare say anything to each other. We just walked with the Khmer Rouge shoving us every now and then. They locked us in an old shed filled with scratchy sacks. My clothes were wet, I was cold, and I was terrified. Chanty was so exhausted he fell asleep, but I could not. What if this was my last night to be alive? I'd already been tortured and beaten up. Would they do more awful things to me, just to watch me suffer? Would they kill my brother? I imagined horrible possibilities all night long. I shook from fear.

When the morning came, a Khmer Rouge yanked us out of the shed.

"We'll see what the boss wants to do with you," he said. "Follow me."

He took Chanty and me back to our settlement to deliver us to the local leader, who would decide our punishment. The leader happened to be away. But what would the guard do? He waited around but seemed to be getting bored. He was annoyed. Finally, he yelled at us and left.

I couldn't believe it. I was alive. Chanty was alive. I felt the terror drain from my body.

We hurried back to Chantha. She had feared the worst. But once again, we had been lucky.

Chapter Six

SURVIVAL

"Am I going crazy?" I asked myself. I was walking along the trail that bordered the rice field where I was working, and I noticed something odd in the shrubs. It looked like a clump of cooked rice, still formed in the shape of a cooking pot. That's exactly what it was! Ants swarmed on it, but I rinsed them off and devoured the rice, the biggest meal I'd had in months.

But one large serving of rice was not enough to keep me alive day after day, week after week, month after month. By winter, my legs and arms were skinny, but my belly looked bloated. I was starving, and I had almost no strength or energy. I felt like a ghost. And then, I got an infection. I was sick with fever. One of my testicles swelled up so large I could not put my pants on. I had seen that happen to other people. They all died.

One morning it was swollen so much that I could not move at all. I felt like I was going to explode. "I'm going to die!" I screamed to Chantha.

Chantha quietly said to Van Lan, but I could hear her, "I think we're losing Mop."

Van Lan turned and said to me in his calm, certain

voice, "We're going to get you well." He was weak too, but somehow he managed to pick me up. He carried me to what we called the hospital, but there was no medicine or doctor. It was just a sagging thatched roof with makeshift beds beneath it. There, a small, white-haired old man tried to take care of the sick people.

He had seen many people just like me. He said, "Eat this. It should help." He fed me something that looked like rabbit droppings. It was probably some kind of scraping from tree bark, some old-fashioned herbal remedy. It did not make me better. I lay there in agony. My whole mid-section throbbed. The person in the bed on my left died. The person in the bed on my right died. I knew my life was about to end, too. The old man said to me, "You are sick because you have eaten nothing but rice chaff for so long."

"I couldn't help it!" I said. "There was nothing else."

"I know," he said. "It's not your fault. But the chaff is not edible, and it's stuck in your intestine. Now it's infected."

He filled a pouch with water and said, "You must promise me you will hold still."

"I will," I said.

Using a stick, he poked the pouch up my rectum. The pouch broke and flooded my intestine. I felt as if that water rinsed out my whole body. My stomach, my intestine, even my testicle, seemed to drain and drain. I fell asleep, and the next morning, I was surprised to discover that I was not dead. The old man looked as startled as I was when I blinked my eyes and smiled at him. I felt better.

"Thank you for keeping me alive," I said simply.

"You're welcome," he answered.

As far as the Khmer Rouge were concerned, every person who was alive needed to work. They didn't care if I had just been really sick. They sent me away from my family, by myself, to work about ten miles from Salatrave. They said a Khmer Rouge would be waiting for me to show up. I knew that if I tried to run away, my family might be killed as punishment. So, I showed up.

When I got there, a Khmer Rouge, holding a rifle, said, "I don't care what you do as long as you guard the corn crop. Don't let the birds eat it. Don't let any animals eat it—and that includes you!"

While I watched for the animals, I sat in a tree so I could be out of the hot sun. Then I heard the rustling of branches close by. A band of about twenty monkeys jumped from a tree into the tree I was in. Dozens of them screamed at me, shook the branches, and charged toward me. Some of them weighed almost as much as I did. Terrified, I leaped to the ground, and they chased me. I ran across the field, which was filled with stumps, remnants of trees that had been burned to clear the land for farming. The stumps scraped against my legs, but I kept going. I must have had a hundred bloody gashes by the time I crossed the field and the monkeys gave up their chase.

The Khmer Rouge didn't care about my wounds. They yelled at me, "You are the enemy! You let the monkeys eat the crop!" I was scared, because that usually meant they were going to kill you. But they just yelled and told me I better not let the monkeys take any more corn.

To protect myself from the bands of monkeys, I made a little shed to hide in. If the monkeys came around, I crouched in my shed and used my slingshot to scare them away. I remembered how Dad and I made monkey traps. Now, by myself, I trapped small monkeys. I pretended Dad was watching me, and if I caught one, I never screamed. To kill the monkey, I choked it with a vine, or beat its head with a stick. I felt awful doing it, but the only other choice was to starve to death. I waited until darkness came before I started a little fire and cooked the meat. I knew I was taking a chance, but when you're hungry, eating is all you can think about. If the Khmer Rouge had caught me, I would have probably died. But if I didn't eat, I would have definitely died.

Sometimes I picked some of the corn for myself. Then I hid it in the jungle. I waited weeks, and when I thought it was safe, I came for it. But early one morning I got caught. The guard yelled at me, "Hey kid, that's not your corn! You are stealing. Come see me tonight."

I lived the rest of that day expecting it to be my last. I was miles away from Van Lan and Chantha, too far to go to them and ask for help, even if they could have given it. I knew that if the Khmer Rouge had to come looking for me, the punishment would be worse, maybe torture in addition to a bullet. Terrified, that evening I went to see the guard as I'd been ordered. If he killed me, my family wouldn't even know what happened. I trembled.

The Khmer Rouge had come close to killing me just a few weeks before. I had been lucky. But had my luck run out?

When he saw me coming, he sneered. He was talking with his friends, and I think he didn't want to be interrupted. In Cambodia, people in the countryside don't sit on chairs. He and the other grown-ups sat cross-legged on the floor. I sat down too, acting as polite and humble as I could. I bowed my head down, staring at the ground. My heart raced. Finally he said, "I don't want to bother with you. Get out of here." He shoved me, and I ran as fast as I could.

My life was spared, but in the weeks to come, people stole food and blamed me. Once I found the shell of a pumpkin and a cucumber peel near where I slept. Whoever took that food wanted to protect himself by making it look like I had taken it. The guard said, "You stupid kid. You just eat, eat, eat, don't you!"

I didn't dare to reply. I lowered my eyes and bowed before him.

"I'm not going to waste a bullet on you," he said. Maybe he knew I hadn't really taken that food because I wouldn't have been so stupid as to leave the evidence close to where I slept. Maybe he didn't think about it at all. I'll never know except that when he might have killed me, he didn't.

At the end of that growing season, when I was fourteen, the Khmer Rouge let me go back to Salatrave. I looked forward to rejoining Van Lan, Chantha, baby Vibol, and my younger brothers. I went to the hut we had built, in a row next to the others. But when I got there, our family's hut was empty. I had no idea where they were. All I could do was wait for them.

Our hut stood at the end of the row, next to a new graveyard that had just been dug to bury all the people who had died from hunger and sickness. That night, I stayed in the hut alone. As I tried to fall asleep, reassuring myself that surely the family would be back the next day, I heard strange noises. They seemed close by. There were clawing sounds, screeches, and grunts. They got louder and more intense. What was it? I didn't believe in demons, but that's what they sounded like. Then, with horror, I realized what they were. Animals of the jungle had come to raid the shallow graves. Wild boars and wolves were digging up the dead bodies and eating what was left of them. They snorted and howled as they gobbled the human flesh.

I lay awake all night, imagining the gruesome scene that I was listening to. Just before dawn, the beasts left, and I finally fell asleep. I awoke when I heard people coming. Was it the Khmer Rouge looking for me, so they could send me somewhere else? The voices got closer, and I recognized the high, sweet sound of Chantha talking. I ran out of the hut and saw my family approaching. Walking next to Chantha, Van Lan carried Vibol. Hackly and Chanty followed a little behind. I had tried hard to convince myself that they had not been buried in any of the shallow graves. And now, here they were.

"Mop!" said Van Lan, smiling and speeding up his pace.

"Oh, dear brother," said Chantha.

If I had not forgotten how to cry, I would have shed tears of joy. Vibol stretched his arms out to me, and I took him into mine. I hugged him and stared with relief at Chantha and Van Lan. Hackly and Chanty seemed even smaller than when we had last been together, their skinny little bodies looking like sticks. Seeing my family made me feel wonderful, but seeing them look so weak and thin made me feel awful. Then Van Lan told me the news.

He said, "Mop, I am so sorry to tell you what we have just found out. Your father's luck has run out."

I knew what that meant.

Chantha said, "He was so smart that for three whole years he managed to stay safe even though the Khmer Rouge wanted to kill him. But in September, he disappeared."

Van Lan said, "Nobody knows for sure what happened, but we have pieced this story together. The Khmer Rouge made one of the men who worked for your father tell him that he had to come out of the jungle. If he didn't, they probably threatened to kill all of us. So, he came out and talked to the Khmer Rouge. They told him they wanted him to cut bamboo for them. He went on their errand, but he never returned. I think he knew what was going to happen, but he sacrificed himself for the family."

It's terrible not knowing what really happened. I heard that Zhen, the fired worker, later bragged that he killed Dad. I don't know if that's true. What I *do* know is that I loved my father.

I will never forget the months we spent together in the jungle. But I don't like popcorn any more, because every time I see it, I think of Dad. And when I see the dawn break and hear birds sing, my chest hurts, because I miss my father. I learned many things in my young life, and one of them was that cruel, greedy people with guns will slaughter good, innocent people. The ones they didn't kill, they starved, tortured, and bullied. There was nothing I could do about it. I had learned that talking was dangerous, so I grieved in silence, alone.

Before the Khmer Rouge came, when I was still a student, learning lessons in school was easy for me. But learning about life's injustice was not.

If my father had evaded the Khmer Rouge for only a few more months, he would likely have been safe.

Vietnam is the country next to Cambodia. A few Cambodian men who had joined the Khmer Rouge were horrifed by the murders they saw. They did not want to continue to be part of the Khmer Rouge, but knew they would be killed if they said so. They went to Vietnam and asked its government to fight against the Khmer Rouge. The Vietnamese government saw an opportunity to extend their power, and they took it. In early 1979, Vietnamese soldiers gained control of Battambang and Phnom Penh. But it was too late for Dad.

Chapter Seven

CROSS FIRE

"The Vietnamese are entering the cities!"
Van Lan told me in a low voice as I was just about to
fall asleep one night. "They will save Cambodia from
the 'saviors.' "

"How do you know?" I asked.

"The freedom news reported it," he said, and I knew
what he meant. We got the news from the radio. Of
course, the Khmer Rouge did not permit anybody to
have a radio. But some of the adults had one anyway.
Without a battery, it was of no use, and nobody had
batteries. But someone managed to rig a battery out of
salt, dried charcoal and a piece of metal. This makeshift
battery worked for about an hour. The adults listened in
the evenings, taking turns to make sure no Khmer Rouge
could hear them. The Khmer Rouge usually camped at
night in the jungle, away from us. Even though having
a radio was risky, Van Lan craved information. Without
it, we were totally isolated. We had no idea what was
happening anywhere else in the country. In whispers, the
adults called the program "freedom news." It was broad-
cast in the Cambodian language from Washington D.C.,

a place that somebody said was in America. When Van Lan told me the Vietnamese were coming into the cities, I was happy. Even though I had never heard good things about Vietnam, it seemed to me having the Vietnamese in charge—anybody but the Khmer Rouge—would be an improvement. Maybe things would change for us, too. But right now, we were far from the cities. In the countryside, the Khmer Rouge still controlled everything.

One afternoon as I walked with some other kids from one rice field to another, I heard the roar of loud engines coming up the road. I hadn't heard the sound of a motor vehicle for years. I actually had been missing the smell of gasoline. Would it be the Vietnamese who might protect us, or the Khmer Rouge who would threaten us? Gunfire opened up. The Khmer Rouge were shooting at Vietnamese tanks. Caught in the cross fire, I hid behind a banana tree and then jumped into a rice paddy. I knew that if I ran, the Vietnamese would think I was a retreating Khmer Rouge and shoot at me. I stayed under water behind a levee until the gunfire stopped. When it was quiet, I cautiously looked up. A lot of people were injured. When I joined my family at the end of the day, I didn't say anything about what happened. I knew that Chantha would be really scared to know that I had almost been shot, so I just kept quiet about it.

We still slept in temporary camps. One day another camp of about a hundred people was set up across the road from ours. The next morning, as usual, I went to work in the rice fields. So did the adults from the new camp. Only old people and very young children stayed behind at the camps.

While I was working in the field, I saw two jets flying low in the sky. They seemed to be heading right at me.

Some other boys yelled, "In the water, get in the water!"

I jumped into the rice paddy and held my breath as long as I could. But I had to come up for air, and then I heard a huge explosion. I ran back to our camp to see what had happened. Vietnamese bombers were probably trying to hit a Khmer Rouge truck parked in the road, but they missed their target. They hit the camp across the road from mine. It was on fire. I saw a girl about my age carrying her younger brother. I asked her, "What happened?" She just pointed to her brother, who had a hole blown through his chest. He was not dead yet, but I knew he did not have long to live.

When the workers from the new camp ran back to their families, I heard their sobs and screams. Almost everybody left in the camp was killed in the bombing— the youngest children, the oldest relatives. Each bomb contained extra explosives that went off after the main bomb exploded. Some workers ran into the camp to see if their families were all right, and the delayed bombs killed them. I heard the screams and smelled the smoke. The next day, nobody wanted to bury the bodies because people were afraid that more of the delayed bombs might go off if the bodies were moved.

As the Vietnamese gained more control in the cities and surrounding areas, the Khmer Rouge chased people like me, and our families, further into the countryside. They did not want their workers to run to the city. They made us march day after day, always away from Battambang. I had no other choice than to move with the group.

The Khmer Rouge planted land mines along the larger roads. They wanted the mines to kill the invading Vietnamese, as well as any Cambodians trying to flee the countryside to head for the cities. One time when the Khmer Rouge made us move, one of them yelled, "Follow us exactly, one behind the other. We know where the mines are, so we know where it's safe. If you step anywhere else, you will be blown up."

My brother Chanty had trouble keeping up. At one point he cried, "Wait for me, wait for me! I have to go to the bathroom." He stepped out of the line, and I was terrified he might put his feet on a land mine. Nothing happened, so I stepped off next to him to see why he was crying. He was bent over in pain. A huge tapeworm was coming out of his body. With my knife, I cut it into pieces as it came out. It was disgusting, and he kept crying. Some of the tapeworm would come out, and then it would slip back in. Chanty would walk a few more yards, and then it would happen again. I don't know how such a big worm could survive in such a small, skinny boy. Somehow he managed to keep moving forward.

I was about to find out that while my thoughts were filled with worries about my brother, Van Lan and some of the other grown-ups were worrying about something else—a huge decision that would affect all of us forever.

Chapter Eight

ESCAPING
THE KHMER ROUGE

Late one afternoon, when we came back from the rice fields to our hut, Van Lan whispered to me, "Go get anything extra to eat that you can, and eat it. Tonight we are leaving!"

Leaving? I hadn't seen any Khmer Rouge order us to move, yelling and waving their rifles at us like they usually did. How could we be leaving? Where were we going? But I held my questions back.

In the darkness that night, about thirty people left with my family. My older brother Bunna had been sent away the year before by the Khmer Rouge. We had seen him only once or twice that year. But now we were together. When we left, he carried a big bag of rice. I don't know how he got it. Van Lan handed me two chickens. "Carry these," he said, so I did.

We walked all night long. I was exhausted. Chantha, Van Lan, and I took turns carrying baby Vibol and helping my younger brothers. Just before dawn, Bunna stepped away from the trail and into the dense jungle. I wondered where he was going. I stopped to wait for him, and then he re-appeared, pushing a bicycle!

"How did you get that?" I asked.

"I saw it out of the corner of my eye," he said. "It was just lying at the base of a tree."

Who knows if the bike had belonged to someone the Khmer Rouge had killed. But no, they would have taken the bike for themselves. Maybe somebody else trying to escape had heard the Khmer Rouge get close, left the bicycle, and run into the jungle.

I would never find out who abandoned that bike, but now, we used it. It was rusty, and one pedal was missing. Bunna tied the bag of rice he had been carrying to the handlebars. The weight made the bike unsteady.

"Help me push it," he said. With my left hand I carried the two chickens, and with my right I pushed the bike seat. Bunna also pushed and guided the handlebars.

I had no idea how long we would be walking, but I knew that if we ran out of rice, we would starve. Bunna and I carried the food that we all needed to survive. We trailed at the back of the group because we were weighted down with the heaviest supplies. I was scared the Khmer Rouge would come up on us from behind, and Bunna and I would be the first ones they would kill.

When morning broke, we finally rested. We were hidden in the jungle, out of sight. I later realized there was no plan, no plotted out route to the city. Our goal was just to stay away from the Khmer Rouge. Every night, we walked again, zigzagging to confuse any Khmer Rouge who might be tracking us. Van Lan decided which direction we should go. I did not ask, "Why are we

I am fourth from the left, posed with some of my siblings during happy times
in Cambodia. From the left, they are Chantha, Lee, Bunna, me, Hackly, and Chanty.
At the time the picture was taken, my oldest sister Chanya had married
and moved away, and my baby sister, Chantu, was not born yet.

During the rainy season, the Cambodian jungle floods. My father and I used vines and hooks to catch fish so we wouldn't starve when we lived together in the jungle, hiding from the Khmer Rouge.

◄◄
This was 1981. I am on the front left posed with other children at the first Thai refugee camp I stayed in. The girl in the white blouse was a volunteer teacher at the camp for a few months. I had found the hat I am wearing, but at the time, could not read the writing on it—U.S.A. I had no idea that one day I would become an American.

►►
Here I am in Oregon City (on the left), playing with three orphans who were born near my hometown of Salatrave. We had not known each other in Cambodia.

Because of the war, I attended school for only a few years in Cambodia. After I came to America, I enrolled in Oregon City High School. I graduated in 1986 after three years of study.

Farmers are planting rice in a field in the countryside. This is similar to what the rice fields looked like in my hometown, Salatrave, when I was a young child.

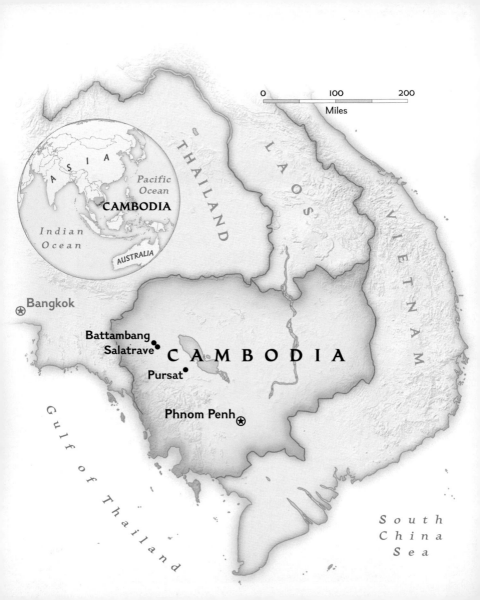

walking this way? How much farther do we have to go? What is going to happen?" It was as if I had blinders on. I just focused on placing one foot in front of another, again and again and again.

We never walked on a road where we would be easy to spot. Open, grassy fields—even if the grass was tall enough to hide us—were not safe either. The Khmer Rouge had put land mines in them to scare people from trying to run away. Instead, we criss-crossed the jungle on narrow, bumpy trails that had been made by small animals. Van Lan studied each path carefully to see if there was any hint of a land mine. He looked for disturbed roots, uneven ground, or anything that might show a mine had been buried there. Barefoot, we stepped as lightly as we could, hour after hour. We took short rests, but we traveled every night, and sometimes during part of the day, too. We were always listening for any Khmer Rouge that might be in the area. To keep the babies in the group quiet, mothers gave them tree bark to suck. It contained a chemical that caused the babies to sleep.

It was the summer dry season, and we were thirsty. I fantasized about the soothing, satisfying taste of water. Then I saw a rise ahead of us. Cambodia is mostly flat, so any ridge really stands out. I knew that during the rainy season, people stay in high and dry spots above the flood plain. They usually dig a well so they can have clear, fresh water to drink. When we got to the high ground, I was thrilled to discover a well there. I looked down into it, and I saw water. My tongue felt even drier than before.

My family stopped to drink. Bunna lowered me into the narrow darkness. I let go with one hand and filled a bucket with water. He pulled me back up, and we drank. But the rest of the group had not waited for our family. We were alone.

When we came out of the jungle, we found ourselves with no clear way to go other than across an open area with high grass, much taller than we were. We had no choice other than to risk the land mines that might be set there. The high grass would hide us from the Khmer Rouge, but we could not see them, either. As usual, Van Lan led the way. I guess he looked at the sun to decide what direction to go. The soil was hot and sandy. My feet burned so much from walking on it that I wrapped rags around them. As the hours passed, the rags shredded. I just trudged along, pushing the bike and thinking about nothing except the miserable discovery I had made—that I could move when I was too tired to move. Then, I snapped out of my thoughts. I spotted what looked like a mound of something, but I could not see clearly what it was. Could this be as valuable a find as the bike? I was still carrying chickens in my hand, so with my foot I tapped the mound. The "mound" leaped up at me! It was a dog. It attacked me and bit my leg. Blood poured out from the wound.

"Van Lan," I yelled. "I'm hurt!"

He stopped and came to me.

"I'll make a bandage," he said. He pulled the shirt off his back and wrapped it around my wound.

"I know you can keep going," he said. "You have to."

As I walked, my leg swelled. I yanked a small branch from a tree and pulled the twigs and leaves off it. Even using that as a crutch, I still could barely move ahead. But somehow, I did.

We walked by day, we walked by night. We rested in short stops, but kept going as much of the time as we could. When we did sleep, we had no choice but to lie down on the ground. When I woke up, I still felt tired. Even the chickens needed breaks. We carried them upside down, and their feet swelled. If they did not walk right side up every now and then, they would die.

A single person could have traveled much more quickly than our family did. We had eaten such poor diets for so long, we were all weak. Hackly and Chanty could not go fast because they were so small. We were all exhausted, but our fear kept us moving.

It was hard to find water. One time we came across a pond, but the water was so muddy it wasn't drinkable. We needed water to cook our rice. Van Lan boiled the water to purify it, but the amount of water was so small in comparison to the dirt that as soon as the water boiled, all that was left was dirt. We walked for many days before we finally came to a good-sized pond of clean water. Alongside it, we saw neat rows of coconut palms and mango trees. There were no houses in sight. The Khmer Rouge must have destroyed the buildings of a small village, and only the trees remained. I was exhausted, and my feet were burned and sore from the hot sand. I was glad that we stayed there for a few days to regain our strength. We ate fruit from the trees, I fished, we cooked rice, and we felt better. Then Van Lan said. "It's time to move ahead again. Let's go."

We met other people trying to escape, too. One man told us that he'd heard the Khmer Rouge caught a group not far away from us. They were all killed.

After three weeks, our zigzagging route brought us closer to Battambang, which we knew the Vietnamese controlled. Van Lan hoped his parents would find their way there, too. Finally, after about a month of walking, we got to the outskirts of Battambang. We were totally worn out. Van Lan asked everyone we met on the road, "Do you know my parents? Have you seen them?" No one had, but we continued into the city.

The first night in Battambang, we were so tired and weak that we just lay down and slept on a sidewalk. The next day, Van Lan met someone who knew his family. He said that they were living in a house by the train station. Van Lan found them. It was a reunion not of joy and celebration, but of exhausted relief. For a short time, Van Lan, Chantha, Vibol, my brothers, and I moved in with Van Lan's parents, sisters, brothers, and their children in a house that had a roof and walls. What a change from sleeping in a primitive hut, or on the ground with no protection at all! I began to feel like a human being again. I was reminded that life might be more than endless work, endless hunger, and endless fear.

Many of the houses in Battambang had been abandoned. People like us who escaped from the Khmer

Rouge looked for an empty house that suited them, and then they moved into it. The house my family found was fairly close to Van Lan's parents'. It needed two new windows, the sink had to be replaced, and the front step had cracked. We made the repairs, and then put a new lock on the door to show that the place was now occupied. That house provided the best living conditions I had experienced for years. It had a flush toilet and, sometimes, even electricity.

"We are free of the Khmer Rouge at last!" I dared to whisper. At least that's what I thought.

Chapter Nine

IN THE CITY

"People here walk so slowly," I said to Ang, Van Lan's nephew whom I'd just met. "This is amazing!"

"Why?" he said.

"In the countryside, the Khmer Rouge made everybody hurry. They made us rush from field to field, or they pushed us as fast as they could to make us go away from the advancing Vietnamese."

Here in Battambang, people were relaxed. They chatted calmly as they strolled the streets. Vendors sold ice that people bought to keep their food cool. I had not seen ice for more than three years. When Chantha asked me to get ice for her, Ang came with me. We were a lot alike. He was just my age. Like me, he was short and skinny. And like me, he was eager to have a friend and to re-learn how to have fun.

After we took the ice to my house, we wanted to go back out and explore more of the neighborhood. We were curious, but one place that we were not allowed to go was the downtown area. Vietnamese soldiers had roped it off to prevent Cambodian people from entering. I think the soldiers grabbed all the valuables, like televisions and radios, and held them there until they could take them to Vietnam.

In the Khmer Rouge-controlled countryside, there was not enough food. But in Battambang, there was plenty of food—that is, for people who had money to buy it. Like many other families who had escaped the Khmer Rouge, we wanted to work, but how could we find jobs? The city was filled with people like us, and we had no way to make a living. Van Lan had an idea. He thought we might be able to make and sell incense to Buddhists, who used it when they prayed. Incense is made from powder. How could we get some?

A few blocks from our house, Vietnamese soldiers were living in a factory that had once been used to produce incense. When I walked by one day, I noticed bags of powder leaning up against the back wall of the building.

I told Ang about them. "Do you want to come with me to try to get some of those bags?"

"You bet," he said.

Hackly and Chanty overheard my question, and they begged to come too. I said okay.

When we got there, we saw soldiers talking and smoking cigarettes by the front door.

"Follow me," I said. I led Ang and my brothers around the side of the building, hoping the soldiers wouldn't notice us.

At the back door, I whispered, "I'm going to open the door as quietly as I can. Follow me in. Grab as many bags of powder as you can, and don't make any noise."

We all sneaked quietly through the back door. The bags of powder were just where I had seen them before, lined up along the back wall away from the soldiers' cots. We each grabbed a bag in both hands. I held the back door open, and one by one we sneaked out of the factory.

At that point, Ang started running. My brothers and I took off too. That's when the soldiers spotted us. They fired their guns, but they aimed way high in the air. They didn't really want to hurt us. They had no use for the powder, so they didn't care if we took it. As we ran, the bags got jostled, spilling clumps of yellow stuff on the ground, on our hands, on our feet, on our clothes. By the time we got back to my house, we were out of breath from running. Panting, we stared at each other. We were covered with powdery yellow splotches. We looked ridiculous! We laughed and laughed. I had almost forgotten what it was like to think something was funny. I laughed some more.

We put all the powder that hadn't spilled into two full bags. Later that day, I handed the bags to Van Lan. I said, "The Vietnamese shot at us, but they missed on purpose."

"Good job," he said. "But we don't want you to be shot at. This is enough incense powder."

I'm not sure what Van Lan did with the powder. As for me, I still wanted to explore, but I knew I should be more careful. I would go into vacant buildings, not ones with soldiers living in them. A couple of days later, Ang and

I came across a building with a sign that said "Theater." The place looked abandoned.

"Should we go inside?" Ang said.

"Sure, nobody's here," I said. I had never seen the inside of a theater before. We cautiously entered through the front door and saw that the building was almost empty. It seemed like lots of people had done the same thing we were doing, taking anything that might help them survive. Then I spotted a small doorway.

"Let's look," I said.

I opened it slowly, and we found ourselves in a dark, little room. It was filled with shelves, each lined with large, round metal containers about two feet across and two inches tall. I wondered what strange things they could be.

I lifted one off the shelf and set it on the floor. Ang helped me pull off the lid, and inside was a metal spool holding a long roll of shiny, see-through material of some kind.

"That's a movie," said Ang.

We pulled it out and unrolled a few feet of it. It was made of pliable plastic, and it had designs in squares pictured on it. Little square-shaped holes lined each edge.

I had no idea the holes were for holding the film onto a projector. If a projector had ever been there, it was long gone. The room was empty except for the rows of canisters. For Ang and me, it was a treasure chest of toys. I held the film up to the light and saw pictures on it, each one almost the same as the next. I slid it between my fingers and saw the scenes slowly change.

"This is a moving picture!" I said.

"Let's really make it move," said Ang.

He pulled the film, foot by foot, from the canister. Then he flung his arm out, and the movie became a curly streamer.

"Let's get up high where we can really let a streamer fly," I said.

We each grabbed a canister and went outside. We spotted a stairway on the back of the building and climbed it to the roof. We sat down and opened our canisters, and then we unwound the film. It was really, really long. As we pulled the film out, it zigged and zagged and curled and seemed alive. I stood up and ran around the roof, holding the film like a kite behind me.

"Over the edge," I yelled.

We whipped our wrists, and the streamers careened from the roof to the lot below. We wiggled our hands and the film danced, twirling from our perch down to the ground.

"Mine's a vine!" Ang said.

"Mine's a snake!" I said.

We shook the film, laughing and yelling. Nobody who watched those movies in the theater could have enjoyed them more than we did that afternoon.

But having fun on one afternoon could not make me forget the reality of my family's situation. We were all torn apart. We did not know where my oldest sister

Chanya was, or what might have happened to her. Was she still in Pursat? And what about Lee? As a student, he had been living with her. Where was he now? Then one day Chanya appeared in Battambang looking for us. I saw her riding a bicycle. I recognized her right away, but she was not the same sister I remembered. When the Khmer Rouge took over Pursat, Lee disappeared. We think they tortured and killed him because he was a student. They also killed Chanya's husband because he was a police officer. Their son died of disease. She suffered an emotional breakdown. When we asked her questions, she barely responded. Speechless with grief for all she had lost, her wits gone, she had somehow managed to find us, but she could barely function. She moved in with us, but the sister I knew had disappeared forever, her mind and spirit broken.

To survive in the city, we needed to find a consistent way to make money. The Vietnamese allowed Cambodians to ride on the Vietnamese soldiers' supply trains for free, as long as they stayed on the roof. Bunna and I rode the train to areas in the countryside that the Khmer Rouge no longer controlled. There, we bought clothing from peasants who made it. Bunna and I sat on the roof of the trains and carried the clothing to Phnom Penh. We sold it there at a profit, and then we brought our earnings back to the family in Battambang. But our business was risky.

Sometimes the Khmer Rouge in the jungle shot at the passing train. When wounded or killed people fell off, the Khmer Rouge took whatever they were carrying. During one ambush, bullets landed all around me, one bouncing off the roof between me and the person crouching next to me. Nothing but luck saved me from getting hit. Van Lan told me the danger was too great, and he told us to stop going. The next week, dozens of people were killed doing just what Bunna and I had done.

My younger brothers and I found a way to earn a little money without riding the train. We made a cart and pushed it into the countryside. With Ang, we picked vegetables and cut sugarcane that had been planted when the Khmer Rouge controlled the area. The Vietnamese had forced the Khmer Rouge out, and now the food was ready to be harvested. Nobody was taking care of the land anymore. The Khmer Rouge had burned down villages and destroyed any system of property ownership. Ripe food in the fields was available for anyone who made the trip to get it—and who was able to avoid the land mines the departing Khmer Rouge had set up. They didn't want "the enemy" to have the food. Next to rice fields and storage barns, they dug holes and put explosives in them. They covered the holes with bamboo and leaves. Unsuspecting people would step on a booby trap, fall into it, and be blown apart.

We picked the vegetables and stayed away from most of the rice barns. We loaded our cart with produce, and then we took turns pushing it back to Battambang. We walked for days. At night, we slept on the ground under the trees. At some intersections, residents left pots of water for travelers to use. One afternoon I saw an old man seated near one of the pots. He asked me questions about where we were going and how old we were. Then he asked to look at our hands. He was a palm reader.

Ang, my brothers, and I each held out our hands for him to study. He said to each of my brothers, "You will stay here in Cambodia." He said to Ang, "Your future is not clear to me. It is a mystery yet to unfold." Then he looked at my palm and said, "Your future is very far away from here. You will tell people about what the Khmer Rouge have done to us."

I had no idea where "far away" might be, but I didn't pay much attention anyway. I did not believe in palm reading.

Chapter Ten

WALKING

"Mop, we want to talk with you," said Van Lan one evening. In a lull between rainstorms, I was playing outside with my younger brothers in front of the house.

I came in and sat down. Chantha was there, too, holding Vibol. He was on the verge of falling asleep.

Van Lan said to me, "Chantha and I want better lives than we can have here. We want more for Vibol, too— and for you."

My heart started pounding. I could tell from his tone of voice that something big was going to happen. I had overheard Chantha and him talking about their frustrations. "There are no opportunities here," Van Lan had said. "What good is our education if there is no work, and the country has no money to rebuild itself?"

Chantha had said, "What kind of future can we give to Vibol? He's only a toddler now, but there will be no school for him, no justice, no future. He won't have a chance."

Then Van Lan said to me, "Chantha and I are determined to escape. There is nothing here for us. Anything of value that the Khmer Rouge did not ruin, the Vietnamese have taken. Would you like to come with us?"

"How can we do it?" I asked.

"We'll use our brains. During these last few months in Battambang, we've worked enough here and there to get a little money. We are strong now, and we can walk as much as we need to. We think you can too. You are brave and you are smart."

I looked down, embarrassed by his generous words.

He said, "We have seen that if you need something, you figure out how to get it. You don't wait for people to tell you what to do or how to do it. You come up with your own ideas. This decision is up to you, Mop. It won't be easy. Although the Vietnamese control the cities and most of the countryside, there are still pockets of Khmer Rouge. And that's not all. The Vietnamese may try to prevent us from leaving, too. They don't want the world to know that we're not happy under their control. Do you want to think about it?"

There was so much to think about, I could hardly think at all. I looked at Chantha. She was still holding Vibol, who had fallen asleep. She stared at me with an anxious expression on her gentle face. At that moment, she looked a lot like Mom.

"Yes, I want to come with you," I said. "What about Bunna and Chanya?"

Chantha said, "Compared to you, Bunna is timid. Van Lan has asked him to help carry Vibol to the border. He has agreed to do it, but he does not want to risk trying an escape. Chanya wants to stay here."

"What about Hackly and Chanty?" I asked her.

"The more people we try to take, the more difficult the trip will be. Van Lan's family wants Hackly and Chanty to stay with them, and I think that is for the best," said Chantha. "And Chanya will be with them, too."

Van Lan said, "We will walk to Thailand, whose name means 'Land of the Free.' Do you know what 'freedom' means? We will have the chance to live every day without fear of the Khmer Rouge. We will be able to find work that we choose and that is worth doing. We will not be hungry. Vibol will have the opportunity to get an education, and to have a future. You will, too."

I had heard fantastic stories about Thailand, but I didn't even know where it was.

"Is it true that there are a lot of luxuries in Thailand— fine food like canned tuna, sodas, and cooking oil?"

"I can't make any promises," said Van Lan. "We will go to one of the Thai refugee camps supported by the United Nations. From there, people move to countries that invite them to come. We think we can get a sponsor who will help us go to France."

We had so few belongings, it didn't take long to get ready to leave. The hardest part was saying goodbye to Ang and to my younger brothers. I told Ang, "Someday we'll meet again, and when we do, we will be in a place where we are free."

"We will not say goodbye. It's 'see you later,' " said Ang.

Hackly and Chanty did not really understand what our going to Thailand meant. I didn't fully understand what it meant, either. Van Lan told them the truth, as simply as he could: "We are going away for now, but we are always one family." Van Lan's family treated my brothers like their own children. They would be safe and loved until they were old enough to make choices about their futures.

During the winter rains the saturated ground was almost impossible to cross, so we waited until the dry summer season of 1980 to begin our long walk to freedom. I was sixteen. We walked and walked, except when we could find a truck driver who would agree to give us a ride for a fee. At night, we slept on the ground.

The Vietnamese soldiers did not want people to leave Cambodia. They wanted the world to consider them our saviors, and if Cambodians fled, then no one would believe the Vietnamese were "saving" us. Traditionally, Vietnamese and Cambodians had not gotten along very well. When the Vietnamese saw an opportunity to gain power in Cambodia, they took advantage of it. But compared to the Khmer Rouge, the Vietnamese were far better. They did not kill people simply because they felt like it.

Along our route to leave the country, we would run across Vietnamese soldiers and use hand gestures to indicate that we lived nearby, since we did not speak Vietnamese. We carried almost nothing with us, so we looked like a family simply returning home from an afternoon's activity, not like what we really were: people running away from their country forever. Without telling me, before we left, Chantha had sewn our valuables inside the soles of our shoes. All she told me was, "It is really important that you always wear your shoes. Do not take them off. Do not lose them. Do you understand?"

I understood.

In the jungle, there was safety in numbers, so some escapees joined together whenever they could. As a large group, we felt less vulnerable to roving bandits. Individuals might join groups, and sometimes, whole families—or what was left of them—would try to come along, too. But we could not really trust anybody. A stranger might be friends with some Khmer Rouge still in the area. We kept to ourselves most of the time, minding our own business and hoping no one would bother us.

Van Lan knew it was not possible for us to walk straight from Battambang to the border. If we heard that any Khmer Rouge were nearby, we changed our route. Van Lan decided where we would go each day. Even if we had to travel in the wrong direction, away from the border, we did it if it meant keeping away from the Khmer Rouge.

I was hot and thirsty, but in the summer, most of the ponds we came across had dried up, looking like nothing more than mud. Parts of skeletons, maggot-filled and decaying corpses, and remnants of clothes floated in the murky swamps. At one point we came to a pond that looked clean. People stood near it, but did not drink. But we were so parched, we gulped the water down. One bystander later told us, "That pond water is contaminated. There are dead bodies in it." We had already drunk the water, so there was nothing we could do. Luckily, we did not get sick.

Later that afternoon, we got caught in a situation that made bad water seem like nothing to worry about. We were walking with about a dozen other escapees along a trail through the jungle. The Vietnamese controlled one side of it, the Khmer Rouge the other. As I trudged along, thinking about almost nothing, I was suddenly shocked into awareness. Gunshots! I didn't see bullets, but I sensed the ringing of them whizzing past us. We all ran in the same direction we had been walking. Bunna, carrying Vibol, was behind me. Everybody was going as fast as they could, and in the commotion, I lost sight of Chantha and Van Lan. My panic pushed me to keep running. By the edge of the trail, I nearly stepped on a dead body. It lay face down, rotting, bloated, and stinking. Horrified, I kept going. Some people stepped on land mines as they ran. The mines exploded and the people were killed.

I don't know how long I ran. It might have been for twenty minutes, it might have been for two hours. I didn't stop running until everything was quiet. Then I walked and watched, focusing on the hope that Van Lan, Chantha, Vibol, and Bunna were safe. The first person I spotted was Van Lan, sitting at the base of a tree. He had made it! Who else was still alive? Van Lan and I waited together, asking any people who came by, "Have you seen our family?" I dreaded their answers, because they might say they had seen their bodies. No one had any news.

Then, Chantha appeared. "Where's Vibol?" she asked. We had no idea. It was impossible to know if he and Bunna had been killed by bullets, blown up by a land mine—or they might be completely safe, looking for us somewhere else on the trail.

"Because Bunna has Vibol with him, he's probably going slowly. It makes sense that they're behind us. Let's wait here for them," said Van Lan.

Van Lan was right. Bunna, carrying Vibol, stumbled upon us. We did not jump up and down, hug each other, or shout with joy. My heart was full, but I had not known true happiness for so long, I did not remember how to express my deepest emotions. Simply, we were together again. We resumed our walk.

As escapees got closer to Thailand, some Khmer Rouge let them pass. They even allowed them to sleep in their camps. Why? I'm not sure. Maybe they wanted people to like them, maybe they felt regret for what they'd done. But they still had guns, and we did not trust them.

We slept one night in a Khmer Rouge camp. We arrived in the dark, so tired that I did not know where we were. Van Lan told me it was okay to go to sleep, so I did. In the morning I awoke in a tent, the kind I had seen the Khmer Rouge use. In shock, I blurted out, "This seems like the Khmer Rouge!" Van Lan clapped his hand over my mouth. "It is!" he said. "But just keep your mouth shut." The Khmer Rouge did not like to be identified by that name. They did not refer to themselves as Khmer Rouge, which meant the "Red Communists."

They called themselves "Angka," which meant "The Organization of Saviors."

We stayed at the camp throughout the day. In the darkness that night, we sneaked away. Then Chantha, Van Lan, little Vibol, Bunna, and I began the last stage of our trek away from our country, toward the unknown.

We walked all night. We crossed muddy streams, got our clothes drenched, and then walked so long that our clothes dried again.

The original plan was for Bunna to return to Battambang once he had helped us carry Vibol to the border. He was going to live with Van Lan's family and Chanya. But now he didn't want to go back. He said, "They don't really need me, and I want to stay with you." So he did.

We were still walking when the sun rose. And then, we emerged from the Cambodian jungle. We saw a well-tended rice field. We had arrived in the Land of the Free!

Chapter Eleven

WAITING

Crossing the border meant little unless we made it into a refugee camp. Van Lan had talked to other people who had tried to escape, multiple times. They told him they had not been allowed to stay in Thailand. Based on what Van Lan learned from them, he warned us, "If we don't get to a camp, the Thai border patrol will send us back to Cambodia." We slept much of the day, resting up before trying to get to a refugee camp under the cover of darkness.

At dusk, we met another group of escapees, and together we hired a guide, someone who made his living helping refugees escape. We came to a paved road that looked deserted, but the guide warned us there might be Thai soldiers in the area. He said, "Some Thai soldiers shoot Cambodian refugees. Some do not." There was no way to tell whether any particular soldier would be our helper or our killer.

One member of our group crawled slowly to the road to listen for cars. He heard none, so we ran as fast as we could across the road. But where was the refugee camp? Someone climbed a tree and saw a mountain in the distance. The guide told us the camp stood at its base. We walked all night long, nonstop, until pre-dawn, when we finally got to the camp. It was fenced. Soldiers watched the surrounding area from tall guard towers. The camp was full and officially closed. Our guide explained, "No more refugees can come in, that is, unless they manage to sneak in."

Before dawn, when it was still fairly dark, our guide said, "At this time, the camp guards might be dozing. But if they are awake, they are probably surveying the distance from the lookout towers." He advised us, "Run, very quietly, close to the base of the tower. If you're lucky, they won't notice you."

That's exactly what we did. After we got past the tower, Van Lan gestured to Bunna to climb the camp gate. He was the tallest, and without too much trouble he pulled himself up and over it. Van Lan helped Chantha climb up it, and Bunna raised his arms to help her on the other side. Next, Van Lan lifted Vibol over and lowered him to Bunna. Finally, he gave me a push, and up and over I went, too. Then Van Lan climbed the gate. We had all made it. Within minutes, I collapsed, asleep on the ground. When I awoke in the daylight, I was surrounded by people staring at us. They were hoping to find their family members among us.

The camp police did not send anyone away who had made it into the camp. It was packed with over a thousand people. We didn't speak Thai, but we understood the camp's name to be "Khao-I-Dang."

Because it was so crowded, my family huddled under a makeshift roof that extended from a shack. Most of the camp structures were ramshackle, thrown together quickly, and then jammed with too many people. People were hungry, and they fought over food. We stayed to ourselves most of the time. There was almost nothing to do, and time passed very slowly. We spent hours playing chess. The chess sets had been made by old men in the camp who whittled wood figurines. There were no jobs, no schools, nothing. There was no joy in this "freedom." Instead, I felt bored and frustrated, waiting and hoping for a sponsor who would allow us to leave the camp. Some people had been waiting for years, and some children knew no other life. My favorite activity was to play with Vibol. He was still learning to talk, and I laughed when he mixed his words up. He was the only one who did not understand our situation.

We heard about other camps that the Thai government used to run but then abandoned. At gunpoint, they made a thousand refugees go back to Cambodia. They forced them in huge groups to move through the mountains and return to the land from which they had suffered so much to escape. Thai soldiers shot old people who could not climb down the steep terrain. Land mines exploded, killing people in the front of the group. People in the back were forced to walk over the dead bodies as the soldiers pushed the group forward. The cruelty of the Thai soldiers shocked the world, and finally the United Nations got involved.

They ran the camp where my family and I stayed.

The rations for Van Lan, Chantha, Vibol, Bunna, and me combined was one chicken every two weeks and one bag of rice for a month. I shouldn't complain, because it was given to us for free. But it was not enough for five people to live on. If you had money, you could buy food. In Thailand, the people eat a lot of noodles, but we never could afford to buy noodles. We lived on rice. If we were lucky, we had a pinch of salt to put on it. We had no meat or fish, but sometimes we cooked the rice in water flavored with tiny shrimp that the camp officials gave us.

Some people in the camps had really, really rich relatives in the United States. They would receive as much as twenty dollars in the mail. Twenty dollars! That could buy everything! The most money I ever had at one time in the camp was one dollar. I bought food with it.

To earn money, I worked in the children's center. Twice a day, I helped distribute United Nations food to the youngest kids. I took Vibol with me every day, so he would get enough to eat. I got food for myself, too, and I took some for Chantha, Van Lan, and Bunna. The cook used to keep water in a barrel that had originally contained cooking oil. He gave the water to me. Before I left the center, I slipped an egg, a vegetable, or piece of fruit into it, and then I'd close the lid so no one could see what I'd done.

For the first time in my life, I watched TV. The

camp had electricity, and sometimes people would pay to watch the TV. I tried to look from outside, but I could not afford the twenty cents they charged to enter. Sometimes they showed movies translated into Cambodian, but usually the TV was in Thai, a language I could not understand.

I had no warning at all before Chantha gave me news that would change my life. "Mop," she said, "I've found a way for you to get out of this camp. You can be the first to go to Paris!"

"What? How?" I asked in disbelief.

"I never told you before, but I have some gold. It's worth one hundred dollars."

"A hundred dollars? You have that much money?" I asked, again finding this hard to believe.

"I've held onto it all these months. Now, I'm using it to buy your freedom," she said. "Van Lan and I have arranged everything for you."

She had given the gold to a woman who lived in a shack near ours. In exchange, that woman promised she would say that I was her son. I was to call her "Mom." She and her children had a sponsor in Paris. Van Lan had a sister in Paris, and he was hoping that she would sponsor them. Chantha tried to reassure me, "You will already be in Paris when we come join you there."

My stomach felt wrenched. I couldn't wait to leave the camp, but I couldn't stand the thought of separating from my family.

Van Lan said, "This is the best plan we can work out."

"Thank you," I said, knowing my words were not enough to convey my feelings. I didn't really even need words. After what we had been through, our understanding went beyond what was said.

I tried to imagine what was going to happen. I had only finished third grade when the Khmer Rouge took over, and I had no idea where Paris was. People in the camp said, "They speak French in Paris, so it's important to learn it." For a few months, a local volunteer came to the camp and gave French lessons. I attended and listened hard when I heard people using French, but we did not have any books, and I learned only a few words.

When "Mom," her daughter, two sons, and I prepared to leave the camp, I was terrified that I would never see my real family again.

"Bon voyage," said Chantha in French, trying to act happy and lighthearted in saying goodbye.

Van Lan said, "Think about what we've survived. This is the final step to true freedom and a future we can make for ourselves. We will see you soon, little brother."

I was so excited, so scared, so upset, I could barely say anything. I told myself that we had been separated many times, and we had always found each other again. I did my best to believe that this time would be no different. I shook Bunna's hand, and I gave Vibol a hug. When my eyes filled with tears, I knew it was time to go.

"Mom's" kids and I were sent to another camp, called

Chunbory. There, all we did was wait to hear whether we had been sponsored. "Mom" had told Chantha that she had a sponsor, but now, that didn't seem to be the case. Her oldest son, who had lived on his own in Phnom Penh, had already passed through this camp before we got there. He had gone to France, but he was not sponsoring us for some reason I did not understand. Every family was on hold, just like we were. When anybody was notified that they had a sponsor, they were really excited and happy. They were going to get out of the camp! Their lives were going to move forward. Everybody acted happy for a family that got a sponsor, but behind their backs, jealous people complained. "Why do they get to go, and we have to stay?"

People said I looked more like "Mom" than her other children did. I didn't tell them the truth about my not being related to her at all. As the weeks and months passed, I missed my real family so much. I had no idea what they were doing, whether they had already left for Paris, whether they'd gotten sick and died, or been sent back to Cambodia. When the Khmer Rouge controlled our daily lives, I had learned more than I ever wanted to know about fear, hunger, and surviving on my own. I was used to the ache in my heart for my mother and my father, but I had filled up the emptiness with love for the family members I still had—Chantha, Van Lan, little Vibol, and my brothers.

Now, even though "Mom" said I was her son, I was not part of that family. I was alone.

All I owned was two pairs of shorts, two shirts, and a towel. Our shack was cramped with twenty people crowded together, so another boy and I slept outside. In the rainy season, I was wet all the time. Our only protection was a small piece of plastic. There were no building materials to make better shelter for ourselves. I spent wet sleepless nights shivering, and I was disgusted by the smell of the nearby sewage drain.

At that camp, my U.N. ration was a chicken a week. I would have starved to death if that was all I ate. Thankfully, religion saved me.

Wealthy Buddhists in the camp used to burn incense and make small food offerings to the gods in the evening. I would sneak over and take any food they left. Sometimes it was a banana, an orange, or even a whole chicken. I'd been warned that food left as a religious offering would poison any thief who took it. But I didn't care, for me that food was not poison. It saved my life.

I no longer believed in God. If there was a god, I knew that he would have had the Khmer Rouge kill me instead of my mother. She had children who needed her, especially our baby sister. My family was Buddhist, but after the Khmer Rouge took over, I stopped believing in any religion. I believed in luck.

From eleven until two o'clock every day, local villagers held an open market next to the camp fence. I had no money, but I hoped to make some at the market. I planned to sell an empty rice bag I had taken and to use the money to buy something nutritious. The bag was worth about a dime. But the camp guards saw me sneak out of the camp with the bag. They ran after me, and they caught me. With big nightsticks, they beat me so badly I slept for more than a day. My body was black and blue, and my head throbbed. I gave up trying to make money at the market.

After we had been in the camp for many months, and for a reason I didn't really understand, "Mom" told me we were not going to Paris after all. I was devastated. My real family was going to France. If I did not make it there, how could I reunite with them? "Mom" said we might go to Canada or the United States. Those names had almost no meaning to me. I had no idea how far France was from the United States or Canada. "Mom" chose the United States, where she said someone else had sponsored her. But the waiting continued. We ended up staying in that camp for a year.

Every day seemed the same as the one before it. There was nothing to do. For a few weeks, a young Thai woman who was studying to become a teacher came to the camp and taught us English as best she could. She came every other day. English is hard to learn! I memorized vocabulary like "apple," "pear," "chair," "cat," "dog," and "floor," but I didn't even learn to say a whole sentence. People with money could pay to watch TV in English, but I didn't have any money or any way to earn it. If I had had books to read or classes to take, I could have improved.

After being sent to another camp, medical examiners

tested us to see if we were healthy enough to emigrate. We were checked for TB and other contagious diseases. One of the examiners told "Mom," "Your family cannot leave because your son is sick." He claimed my scars from the bullet wounds were actually signs of disease.

We felt angry and frustrated, but I could do nothing about my scars. I hated to cause problems. I worried constantly. Other families left, but we were stuck there. For three more months, we waited. "Mom" and her sons were mad. "It's because of you that we have to wait!" they said. When food was short, I was left out. They hoarded their food and ignored me. But the little sister, Kuntiya, who was about seven years old, felt sorry for me. Sometimes she shared her food as if I were her real brother.

Over the next months, my scars did not change, and finally the doctor was persuaded that my bullet wounds would not hurt anyone else. He signed our papers.

We were moved to another camp, called "Lupini." I think the facility used to be a jail. The walls were high, there were no windows, and it was even more crowded than the camps where we had been living. We spent two weeks there. Then we got the news: "In two days, you will leave for America." We were so excited and nervous we could barely function. When a huge vehicle barreled into camp and we were told to get on it, I didn't know if I could make myself do it. I had never seen anything so big. The mini-vans used as buses around Battambang were tiny compared to this monster bus. But everyone leaving the camp got on it, and I did too. During the 20-minute drive to the airport, my heart raced.

At last, we were about to journey to the other side of the world.

Chapter Twelve

FLIGHT TO FREEDOM

I had seen airplanes in the sky before, but had never been close to one. That changed on a morning during the winter of 1982. I don't even know the exact date, but I will never forget how I felt as I walked toward that plane. I thought, "This is amazingly, incredibly, impossibly huge! There's no way this giant machine will ever fly." Then I stepped onto the plane's stairs, lifting myself away from the ground, away from Asia, away from everything I had ever known. I was eighteen years old.

My heart raced. I wasn't winded from climbing the long flight of steps. I felt out of breath with the excitement of what was happening. I was released from the jail of the refugee camps. I was at last, at long last, going to be free of them. But my heart felt heavy. I was going away from my family—maybe. I didn't know where they were, or even if they were alive. Were they still waiting in a camp? Had they made it to France? I knew I was not going to France. I didn't care where I lived, if only I could be with them.

This plane was bound for San Francisco, California, U.S.A. I memorized the destination, but I knew nothing about it.

After the plane succeeded in taking off, I had to admit anything was possible. I looked out the window and saw dark green jungles interrupted by flat patches of rice fields. Then we were flying through clouds. My head felt cloudy, too. We were given food—lots of it. It was the first time I'd ever eaten American food. I absolutely loved it. I didn't know the names for any of it, but I especially liked what I later learned was called canned fruit cocktail. It was delicious. "Mom" and her kids were air sick the whole flight, but I felt fine. I had no idea what lay ahead, but I knew I liked having plenty of delicious food to eat.

I did face one problem. After many hours on the flight, after I had been eating and drinking, I needed to use a bathroom. I had no idea what to do. I watched people go in and come out of a small room at the back of the plane. They probably wondered what I was staring at. I decided to investigate that room. I figured out what to do there, but I was completely amazed. Where did the water come from, and when the toilet flushed, where did the water go?

When we landed, I did not know what to expect. What would it be like in San Francisco, California, U.S.A.? When the plane came to a standstill, the passengers squeezed into the plane's aisle, practically pushing against the door to get off. The pilot stood by the cockpit and smiled at us as we filed out. I smiled back at him. But when he looked at me, he acted like he was shivering and held his arms around himself as if he were cold. I wondered why. Then I found out. I was wearing the only clothes I owned, a pair of shorts and a shirt. I did not realize how incredibly cold it would be outside. When I got off the plane, I nearly froze! I had never experienced such cold before.

I don't think any of the refugees who got off that plane knew what to do. I was too polite to ask "Mom" what was happening, and I suspect she wouldn't have known anyway. I simply followed her into the terminal. It was the tallest, widest, brightest building I had ever seen. Where should we go? None of us could understand English. Some people smiled at us and gave us each a ham sandwich. Mine was wonderful! Everybody else in "Mom's" family still felt sick from the plane ride. They didn't want their sandwiches, so I ate them. I would have been happy to eat ham sandwiches for a year.

Folding chairs had been set up for us inside the terminal. Nobody used them. Most of the people who had been on our plane lay down on the floor to sleep. "Mom" saw a large, beautiful sculpture, and we decided it might be safe to sleep next to it. We did. Now I know what the "sculpture" was. It was a garbage container.

"Mom" had told me that our sponsor lived in Salem, Oregon—wherever that was. He was a Cambodian doctor whose family had all died. He tried to help other people. How would we get to Salem? I felt a new kind of fear. I was used to the guns and cruelty of the Khmer Rouge. I was used to hunger. I was used to missing my family. But now I was in a completely foreign place packed with people who did not look like me and whose language I did not understand. I felt completely lost.

Finally, a man who spoke Cambodian talked to our group of refugees. He said, "Welcome to America! I am sorry you have been without a guide, but I am here now. Together we will take a bus to your temporary housing. You'll be there for two or three days, and then you will go to your final destinations."

He escorted our group to the most colorful bus I'd ever seen. It was silver, with blue and red stars and lettering painted on it. We climbed aboard and rode through the city streets. They were crowded with cars and trucks of all shapes and sizes. The people on the sidewalks looked tall and healthy. They walked briskly, alone or in pairs. Many of them carried leather or plastic bags. They wore coats, and a few wore hats. I marveled at their hair—blond, brown, black, and gray—sometimes straight, sometimes curly. I'd never seen such variety. We weren't on the bus long, but I felt like I'd taken in a month's worth of new sights. Then the bus stopped, and our guide told us to get off at our dormitory. It was really nice.

Like the other refugees, on the first day in the dormitory I was handed a thick parka and a pair of brown leather shoes. They were used, but I didn't care. For all of us, these were wonderful gifts. We really needed those clothes, especially at night. They kept us warm. Nobody explained to us that if we were cold in our rooms, we could turn a heater on. In Cambodia, it is never cold, so we had never seen a heater. We did not know the purpose of the dials and boxes on the wall of our room. We were afraid to touch them.

One of the boys in the family took a shower. He said to me, "It was cold! I almost froze to death!" I went to investigate. When I turned the knob, I almost got burned to death. But I figured out the trick. We had to turn on both faucets to balance the hot and cold.

When it was time to eat—to get free food—I was usually first in line. I would pick up a tray and then select from a long counter packed full of foods. They looked like nothing I had eaten before. I tried something different for each meal. On the last morning, I saw something familiar—a bunch of bananas. We had bananas in Cambodia. "They must have everything here," I thought.

On the third day, we were loaded onto the fanciest bus I had ever seen. I laughed at myself for having thought the bus that took us from the camp to the airport in Thailand was deluxe with its padded seats, matching upholstery, and bright paint. I was impressed by this bus, but I was amazed by the driver. It was a woman! I had never seen a woman drive a car, much less a bus. My brain was whirling.

More surprises awaited me. We approached the biggest bridge I had ever seen. Someone told me it was called the Golden Gate, but it wasn't gold. It was dark red. No matter what its name was, how could a bridge be so long? We got closer and closer to it, and I realized we were going to drive onto that bridge. I couldn't believe it. We crossed that enormous span, riding in a huge bus, driven by a woman. "This country is amazing!" I said. I had never seen, experienced, or even imagined anything like it.

Eventually we boarded a plane to Portland, Oregon. From there, we got on another flight to Salem. I had survived the Khmer Rouge and the camps in Thailand. I had flown over the Pacific Ocean. I had crossed the Golden Gate Bridge in a bus driven by a woman. But I thought I would be killed on the tiny plane from Portland to Salem. It held only about twelve people. It flew really low, and the ride was very bumpy. On that flight, for the first time in my life I saw a fat person. Nobody in Cambodia was fat. He took up two seats. I thought his weight would make the plane crash.

To my great relief, in spite of that oversized man, we landed safely. The flight attendant opened the door, and I got in line to exit the plane. As soon as I stepped outside, I inhaled the crisp air, tinged with the smell of jet fuel. I saw people busy at work around me. Some of them wore bright orange uniforms. They were unloading baggage from the plane. Others were driving trucks that pulled trailers filled with suitcases. Everyone looked big, strong, and energetic. I thought, "These people eat three meals a day. This is a land of prosperity and opportunity. And I am here."

I climbed down the airplane's stairs and stepped onto the ground. At that moment, I knew that I was truly beginning my new life in the United States of America. I felt scared, but excited. For the first time, I looked forward to making my own future.

AFTERWORD

Nawuth wasted no time in building a life of his own in the United States. At first he lived with "Mom" and her children. He was given a monthly welfare check of $300, and he got a job working as a dishwasher for $3.17 an hour. He gave "Mom" all his money. At home he worked, too, cleaning up the house and doing the dishes while the other kids had fun. He felt like the family's servant.

When he learned that Chantha, Van Lan, Vibol, and Bunna were living in a refugee camp in Indonesia, he asked "Mom" for ten dollars of his earnings to send to them. But "Mom" refused. Enraged, he left "Mom" and moved in with his great aunt, whom he had discovered lived not too far away, in Oregon City.

In 1983 he wanted to enroll in the local community college to improve his English, but the counselor advised him to go to high school instead. He felt like an orphan with no identity, so he created his own. He enrolled using a name he chose for himself, Nawuth (NA-wooth.) In Cambodia he had attended school for only a few years. In spite of his lack of formal preparation, he graduated from Oregon City High School with an "A" average in only three years.

He married his high school sweetheart Rany Prak, also a Cambodian immigrant. They moved from Oregon to San Jose, California, to be near her mother. At San Jose City College, Nawuth completed a certificate program as a machinist. He found employment as a machinist during the day, and he worked the night shift at a donut shop, too.

Nawuth and Rany (who now goes by "Kelly") have three children—Brian, Anthony, and Stephanie. Nawuth tells them, "Nobody loves you like your parents do. I know because I've lived in situations where I never got the love that you know you can count on."

Chantha, Van Lan, Vibol, and Bunna made it to France. They settled in the city of Lyons. So did Van Lan's nephew, Ang. Since then, the family has stayed in close touch, and they have visited each other's homes on opposite sides of the globe.

Still in Cambodia, Nawuth's oldest sister Chanya remarried and had three children, now grown. Her husband left her and then died in an accident. Chanya works in a military hospital in Pursat.

Chanty, Nawuth's youngest brother, went to France to live with Van Lan and Chantha but then returned to Cambodia. He got married, and he and his bride moved to Stockton, California, about an hour away from Nawuth. They have one son.

Van Lan told Nawuth that he heard from friends in Salatrave that Zhen and his son built a house on the spot where Nawuth's family used to live. Zhen's son lives there now.

In 2004, Nawuth bought a ticket to America for Hackly, who suffers from chronic medical problems. In Cambodia he got very sick from eating pork that was not properly cooked. The disease affected his brain, and he suffers from seizures. Now he's living with Nawuth and getting treatment. To simplify his name, people call him Lee.

In 2007, Nawuth and Kelly moved to Hollister, about 25 miles (40 km) south of San Jose, where they bought a bagel shop. Lee helps them as much as he can. Nawuth has kept his machinist job, too, about an hour and a half away. With the long commutes and the two jobs, most nights all he can get is five hours of sleep. "I work seven days a week," he says, "but I have no complaints."

When Nawuth bought a new car not long ago, he said a friend complimented him on it and asked, "Did you always dream of coming to America and driving a new car?" Nawuth chuckled and explained, "When I lived in Cambodia, nobody in my village dreamed of having any car at all. At one point, my dream was to have three meals a day, and then to have even one solid meal a day. I had no idea I would come to the United States. I never could have predicted all the things that would happen to me." Then he added, "or all the things that I would be able to make happen."

Nawuth knows what freedom means.

Time Line of Khmer Rouge Occupation and More

1962
Pol Pot becomes Secretary General of Cambodian Communist Party.

1964
Nawuth Keat is born in the small village of Salatrave, Cambodia. He is the fifth of Seang and Thy Keat's eight children.

1965
Cambodian King Norodom Sihanouk breaks off relations with the United States because he fears he will be removed from power. He allows North Vietnamese rebels to set up bases in Cambodia to fight the U.S.-backed government in South Vietnam.

1968
Pol Pot becomes the leader of a rebel group. He is forced to flee into the Cambodian jungle to escape King Sihanouk. While living in the jungle, Pol Pot forms a movement that becomes the Khmer Rouge. They wage a rebel war against the Cambodian government.

1970
King Sihanouk is removed from power by a U. S.-backed military coup. The Khmer Rouge republic is created. The Cambodian Prime Minister, General Lon Nol, takes power.

EARLY 1970S
The Cambodian army begins losing territory to the Khmer Rouge and Northern Vietnamese.

1973
The Khmer Rouge attacked Salatrave, Nawuth's hometown. Nawuth and his family try to flee, but are caught. Five members of his family are killed. Nawuth is shot three times, but he survives.

1975
Prime Minister Lon Nol is overthrown and the Communist Khmer Rouge, led by Pol Pot, take over Cambodia's capital, Phnom Penh. They immediately begin evacuating people from towns and cities to create a society based on farming. City residents are forced to the countryside to work the land. Former King Sihanouk briefly becomes head of state again.

1976
Cambodia is renamed Democratic Kampuchea. King Sihanouk resigns and Khieu Samphan becomes head of state with Pol Pot as Prime Minister.

1977
Nawuth is living in a group hut and working in the rice fields of Salatrave with his younger brothers. Sometimes his sister Chantha and her husband Van Lan work nearby.

DECEMBER 1978
Vietnam invades Cambodia after Khmer Rouge rebels continually cross the border. The Cambodia-Vietnam War begins and the Vietnamese remove the Khmer Rouge from power, driving them into the countryside.

JANUARY 1979
Vietnamese troops take over Phnom Penh, drive Pol Pot to the border of Thailand, and begin their ten-year occupation of Cambodia. The People's Republic of Kampuchea is created.

1979
Escaping the Khmer Rouge who still control the countryside, Nawuth and his family flee to Battambang.

SUMMER 1980
Chantha, Van Lan, Vibol, Bunna, and Nawuth walk to Thailand.

WINTER 1982
Nawuth boards his flight to the U.S. and to long-awaited freedom.

1989
The last Vietnamese troops withdraw. The country is renamed Cambodia.

1993
Free elections are held in Cambodia. The Khmer Rouge boycotts them. King Norodom Sihanouk returns to the throne after a new constitution brings back the monarchy.

1996
The Khmer Rouge movement is weakened when high-level Khmer Rouge begin breaking their allegiance to the party.

1997
The Cambodian government asks the United Nations to put Khmer Rouge leaders on trial for their crimes. Pol Pot is ousted as Khmer Rouge leader.

1998
Pol Pot dies. His death signals the end of the Khmer Rouge.

1999
The last Khmer Rouge surrender.

2001
Cambodia passes a law to create a court dedicated to trying members of the Khmer Rouge for the crimes they committed when in power.

2004
King Sihanouk abdicates the throne.

2009
Khmer Rouge trials begin.

Illustration Credits

COVER: A modern Cambodian boy in Phnom Penh carries a basket similar to one Nawuth carried as a child: Mak Remisa/epa/Corbis
INSERT: All photos courtesy of the author, unless otherwise noted below
Jungle: Khoroshunova Olga/ Shutterstock
Rice field: Corinne Martin/ iStockphoto

 Founded in 1888, the National Geographic Society is one of the largest nonprofit scientific and educational organizations in the world. It reaches more then 285 million people worldwide each month through it's official journal NATIOAL GEOGRAPHIC, and its four other magazines; the National Geographic Channel; television documentaries; radio programs; films; books; videos and DVDs; maps; and interactive media. National Geographic has funded more than 8,000 scietific research projects and supports an education program combating geographic iliteracy.

For more information, please call 1-800-NGS LINE (647-5463) or write to the following address:

National Geographic Society
1145 17th Street N.W.
Washington, D.C. 20036-4688 U.S.A.

Visit us online at www.nationalgeographic.com/books